Best practice tendering for Design and Build projects

Alan Griffith
Andrew Knight
Andrew King

┳┳ Thomas Telford

EPSRC

D0316209

Published by Thomas Telford Publishing,
Thomas Telford Ltd, 1 Heron Quay, London, E14 4JD.

www.thomastelford.com

Distributors for Thomas Telford books are:
USA: ASCE Press, 1801 Alexander Bell Drive, Reston, VA 20191-4400, USA
Japan: Maruzen Co. Ltd, Book Department, 3-10 Nihonbashi 2-chome, Chuo-ku, Tokyo 103
Australia: DA Books and Journals, 648 Whitehorse Road, Mitcham 3132, Victoria

First published 2003

A catalogue record for this book is available from the British Library

ISBN: 0 7277 3218 8

© Thomas Telford Limited, 2003

Throughout the book the personal pronouns 'he', 'his', etc. are used when referring to 'the client', 'the contractor', etc. for reasons of readability. Clearly, it is quite possible these hypothetical characters may be female in 'real-life' situations, so readers should consider these pronouns to be grammatically neuter in gender, rather than masculine.

Typeset by Alex Lazarou, Surbiton, Surrey
Printed and bound in Great Britain by MPG Books, Bodmin, Cornwall

Preface

Best practice tendering for Design and Build projects is based on the detailed findings of an Engineering and Physical Sciences Research Council (EPSRC) project (Knight *et al.*, 2002), focusing explicitly on Design and Build (D&B) tender evaluation. D&B is perhaps the most popular form of integrated procurement route that has been increasingly adopted both in the UK and overseas in recent years. This synthesis of design and construction activities has the potential to lead to more efficient supply chain solutions. The increased popularity of D&B can be understood when one considers the advantages it offers over traditional contracting, for example, single point responsibility, shortened project time-frames and buildability. The D&B term covers a range of different procurement options, the variety of which brings unique risk and design distribution patterns. The book seeks to reduce confusion over the terms often used to describe different approaches by suggesting an easily communicable *continuum* of D&B variants.

D&B tendering is widely reported as different to tendering on traditional construction projects, as it requires the employment of mechanisms to account for differentiation in contractors' bids. Although differentiated from traditional tendering, there is a lack of detailed guidance for practitioners involved in the preparation of tender mechanisms, especially the evaluation aspect. The inability to utilise best practice techniques and develop clear aims for the evaluation process leads to an overuse of time and resources, in addition to the possibility that the selection process is not able to select the contractor offering the best value bid. Ultimately, inefficiency in this important element of the procurement process places upward pressure on prices in the industry.

This book examines tender evaluation strategy from both supply and demand sides of the construction industry, presenting an understanding of the concepts and issues involved. It provides clear guidance allowing those involved in the construction procurement process to implement a range of tendering mechanisms suitable for the various types of D&B in use today. More consistent and effective application of suitable tender methodologies can reduce the time, resources and costs of the tendering process, thereby providing greater efficiency and effectiveness in construction.

Alan Griffith
Andrew Knight
Andrew King

Acknowledgements

The work embodied in this book was reviewed by a panel of expert practitioners who are involved in various aspects of the UK construction industry. Their dedication, time and effort are gratefully acknowledged.

Geoffrey Minshull, MSc FCIOB FRSA
John Mowlem and Company plc

Martin Pitt, LLB MRICS
Bluestone plc

Paul Stokes, FInstCES
South Kesteven District Council

We would also like to thank all those, both in the UK and overseas, who contributed to the research project on which this book is based. Particular thanks are given to the following:

Professor Craig Capano, AIC CPC
Milwaukee School of Engineering

Allan Day, BEng CEng MICE
BAE Systems

Deborah Poodry
Massachusetts Institute of Technology

Professor Randy Rapp, PE CCE AIC
Milwaukee School of Engineering

Clare Sneyd, BSc MCIPS
Boots Properties plc

Brian Swenson, PE
HNTB Group of Companies

Contents

Chapter 1

Introduction

This book is based on an Engineering and Physical Sciences Research Council (EPSRC) project focusing on Design and Build tender evaluation. The project was undertaken in the School of Environment and Development at Sheffield Hallam University over a three-year time-frame and was graded 'tending to internationally leading'.

A report undertaken by the Government appointed Construction Task Force (Egan, 1998) highlighted several areas of concern in the UK construction industry. A central theme in the document is industry underachievement in meeting customer needs. One fundamental change considered necessary is to refocus the construction process on the end consumer rather than the next employer in the supply chain. However, a reduction in the level of fragmentation and an increasingly integrated construction process would be required to facilitate these changes. One approach to reducing these problems in the supply chain is the procurement process known as Design and Build (D&B). Allowing an organisation to produce a design and then build a project has the potential to lead to a more efficient solution. However, the selection of a contractor under D&B is more difficult than under a traditional contract. This is because a variety of factors need to be evaluated including many variables that are difficult to quantify, for example the quality of aesthetics.

There are a variety of publications that discuss the advantages of D&B. Nevertheless, there is a lack of detailed guidance for practitioners involved in the preparation of contract documents and tender evaluation mechanism(s). Therefore, this book specifically addresses the area of tender evaluation and aims to provide guidance for those involved in the process. The research project on which this book is based examined evaluation strategy from both the supply and demand sides of the industry. This allows areas of best practice to be disseminated to members of the construction industry, including clients. The potential benefits include a more efficient procurement process leading to greater client satisfaction.

This book draws on the key lessons derived from the EPSRC research project and satisfies the following needs.

(*a*) Clear guidance for the design and real-life application of D&B tender mechanisms. This is aimed at providing those involved in the procurement process with a range of different tendering mechanisms able to be used on the varying types of D&B found in use today.

(*b*) Reduction in resource usage and the associated costs of tender process. Studies have shown that much needless waste can occur in tendering; more consistent and effective application of tender methodologies can achieve efficiency savings and aid identification of the most suitable project teams.

(*c*) To procure in a best practice manner. There is increasing pressure for clients to procure construction projects using best practice initiatives. This book addresses the often-cited need to select contractors on the basis of best value and provides justification for various strategies.

(*d*) Reduce confusion over the terms used to describe various different approaches to D&B procurement. This book suggests an easily communicable continuum of D&B, which is based on the differing amount of pre-contractor design and specification development. These clear definitions present a basis for informed usage as they take account of the reasons different variants are being used by practitioners in industry.

A triangulated grounded theory methodology was utilised in the project. The advantage of this methodology is that it allows issues to emerge based on their relevance to the topic under study. These emergent themes may not have been recognised if a traditional hypothetico-deductive logic were employed (Strauss and Corbin, 1998). The triangulated design utilised a focus group, a three-phase series of semi-structured interviews, and a postal survey. The focus group was used to initiate data collection and took place with the project partners, who represent both the supply and demand sides of the industry. Semi-structured interviews were undertaken with a range of clients, consultants, contractors and academics over the three-year project period. The interview sample purposefully focused on a range of organisations, differentiated by their size and specialism, to adequately represent the different applications of D&B. The interview data were indexed and analysed using Qualitative Software Research (QSR) Non Numerical Unstructured Data Indexing Searching and Theorising (NUD*IST 5) software in addition to Banxia Decision Explorer software. The analysis followed a predetermined structured path and resulted in 953 open categories, in addition to the development of 60 conceptual categories. This level of precision in data modelling resulted in a highly refined database open to repeat and varied interrogation. Throughout the book quotes from interviews with participants are used to highlight pertinent issues. In addition, where relevant, the historic development of various concepts are presented to locate the work in a wider context. Owing to the international nature of the text, the terms 'tender' and 'bid' are used interchangeably.

The book's content is separated into six main chapters, which are structured to allow the reader to stay focused on their particular area of interest. The six main chapters present the following issues.

Chapter 2 — Design and Build

This chapter introduces the reader to the key concepts of D&B procurement. More experienced practitioners may select to bypass this section and access their specific areas of interest in the text. Nevertheless, the basic concepts in D&B are presented, including various findings from the research project on which this book is based. Beginning with a definition of D&B and its differentiation from traditional contracting, it proceeds to consider the historic origins of D&B, showing that, paradoxically, it precedes 'traditional contracting'. The generally accepted advantages and disadvantages of this procurement route are presented prior to a discussion of the D&B continuum. The continuum of pre-contractor design and specification development has been developed from the project data and allows a common basis for differentiating the various types of D&B found in use. The movement towards more developed forms of D&B are acknowledged, and the reasons for this change presented. The increasingly detail-developed types of D&B impact on the type of tender competition being used in practice and should, therefore, be considered an important element of the D&B selection process. With the exception of integrated supply chain development, the rationale for more detail-developed forms of D&B are aimed at isolating the scheme design and specification from contractor involvement and, as such, are more in tune with traditional contracting than with the pure view of D&B.

Novation is an increasingly popular legal mechanism that is used in conjunction with D&B, and a section of Chapter 2 focuses on the issues involved. Despite the popularity of novation with clients and their consultants, founded mainly on the belief that it protects the client's interests, the overall conclusion is that clients should take a more balanced view of the advantages and disadvantages of novation before they decide to incorporate it in their procurement path.

Short-circuiting in D&B projects describes the process where, for various reasons, the architect working for the contractor interacts directly with the main building client to develop the design and specification. This activity can ultimately result in the client being dissatisfied with the end building product, as their expectations may not be matched by the contractor's actual development of the scheme. Short-circuiting is the subject of the final section of this chapter.

Chapter 3 — The development of tendering arrangements in the construction industry

This chapter deals with the key principles involved in tendering practice. It begins with a brief evolutionary journey through the key UK reports that have contributed to the current state of contractor selection. In doing so, it introduces such concepts as open tendering, which has been widely derided for various reasons including the selection of unsuitable contractors who tendered unrepresentatively low bids. The move to selective approaches, which lie at the centre of current practice, are discussed.

The Highlight Optimum Legitimate Tender (HOLT) technique is presented briefly, as it shows a detailed methodology for tendering that is based on empirical evidence of the problems inherent in selection processes (Holt, 1995).

Open-, single- and two-stage selective, serial and negotiated tendering approaches are then expanded to allow a greater understanding of the nature of these key tendering principles.

Chapter 4 — Pre-qualification

Focus then shifts to the pre-qualification process, which lies at the heart of the majority of tender processes currently used. Pre-qualification can be considered as a filter process, and is used to identify contractors who are suitable to tender for projects. Literature showing major works in the field are discussed, and they focus on the advantages of pre-qualification and the kind of problems that have been shown to ensue where it is not used.

The EPSRC study data show how contractors often view the process negatively, something that is often based on their belief that the process is overly bureaucratic. This view is contrasted with the client's clear need for relevant information, particularly up-to-date financial information allowing necessary selection decisions to be made.

The work of Palaneeswaran and Kumaraswamy (2001) highlights various approaches to pre-qualification that are used worldwide; approaches that practitioners may find useful in shaping their own practices. An area of best practice identified in the EPSRC study is that of the 'reality check'. This describes the activity whereby clients and their consultants actively test potential contractors to gauge whether the corporate message forwarded in presentations relates to the reality of the contracting organisation.

Chapter 5 — Competition in Design and Build projects

Following the pre-qualification process, the focus shifts to consider the view of the D&B tender design competition and how this often-reported practice is decreasing in use. The increasing use of detail-developed forms of D&B accounts for more straightforward tender evaluations, with lowest capital cost and compliancy being the most important decision criteria, as opposed to the multiple criteria often utilised in the D&B design competition. The move toward detail-developed forms of D&B have resulted in contractors being given an increasingly limited role in D&B, with their input often being limited to construction in a similar way to traditional contracting. The argument to increase contractor involvement from as early stage as possible is forwarded, thereby allowing D&B to fuse the design and construction process as originally intended.

Value is often mentioned as the ideal focal point of best practice selection mechanisms. Instead of simply repeating this often misunderstood rally cry, the nature of value is discussed to allow more careful consideration. To develop an understanding of the term value, the core concepts of *value in exchange* and *value in use* are used to allow the reader to gain purchase on these elements of economic theory. Following consideration of whether value can actually be measured, we concentrate on value in a construction tendering context. Various reports have shown the overriding use of lowest capital cost in contractor selection. However, these findings, including that of this study, show practice is often unrelated to the widely voiced calls to select all members of the project team on the basis of best value. This book aims to provide practical tools to allow best value selection based on empirical data. However, in contrast to many other publications, this book adopts a pragmatic stance and acknowledges that many clients do not select on a best value basis. By presenting various different selection mechanisms, those involved in the selection process can make informed decisions regarding their own practice.

Value management is often quoted as an example of the type of activity that should be undertaken to improve the procurement process. While this is undoubtedly true, the study has shown that there is significant confusion over what value management actually entails. This book aims to clarify the value management process in D&B by presenting in clear and simple terms its key components in Chapter 5, while an example of a value management study, and its application in the selection process are presented in Chapter 7.

Alternatives are an essential part of the D&B tender process as they allow contractors to input into schemes that are often very well developed prior to being tendered on. The need to take alternatives seriously is stressed, with a form of menu pricing being useful in structuring the submission and evaluation of alternatives.

Chapter 6 — Published guidance, ethical and practical considerations

Tendering codes of practice that are commonly applied in industry are discussed in Chapter 6. These include various National Joint Consultative Committee (NJCC) documents that are still found at the centre of many tender processes despite the NJCC no longer being in existence. In addition, the Construction Industry Board (CIB) code of procedure (CIB, 1997) and recent Joint Contracts Tribunal (JCT) *Practice Note Six* (JCT, 2002) are discussed. Craig's (2000) criticism of the NJCC and CIB codes is used to show the complex dynamics at play with regard to both irregularities and errors, and qualified bids.

Ethics are an important issue in tendering, as Friedman (1982) and Ray *et al.* (1999) have shown. The work of Ray *et al.* is drawn on to show the importance of issues such as the withdrawal of bids, bid cutting, cover pricing, compensation of tendering costs, and collusion. An ethical issue specific to D&B is the dissemination of the Contractor's Proposals. In D&B, clients are in a position to intentionally trade information between contractors for their own gain. Although this is an ethical consideration, it also involves legal implications such as copyright. The client and their consultants may also unintentionally disseminate the Contractor's Proposals as part of their interaction with various tendering contractors. This is a practice that should be curtailed as much as possible.

D&B is sometimes regarded as offering the potential to allow contractors to decrease the quality of specifications to maximise their profit. Drawing on the views of US authors, the logic of this view is challenged. Nevertheless, many architects interviewed as part of the project subscribed to such a view and underpinned it with their belief that contractors were not professionals. Again, this view is challenged, and the reality that many contractors belong to organisations that require them to operate under ethical frameworks is forwarded. The chapter concludes by considering some practical considerations of tender costs and the decision whether or not to use a competitive procedure.

Chapter 7 — The practical application of best practice tendering

This chapter builds on the key principles laid out in previous chapters. It develops these principles to provide a basis for formulating a selection process. The three main types of D&B that were developed in Chapter 2, pure D&B, partially developed and detail-developed — form the basis of different types of tender competition. Various dynamics of the tender process follow, which include an extension of the issues first raised in Chapter 5 concerning selecting on lowest capital cost or best value. For example, tender competitions that require scheme development from contractors should ideally utilise selection mechanisms that allow the differences to be evaluated in a structured manner. An example of the various different stages of a value-management study are presented, highlighting its usefulness in establishing client objectives and tender evaluation.

Despite being only one small component of a building's total costs over time, capital cost often forms the basis of selection. The whole-life costs of facilities should ideally form the basis of selection and, with this in mind, the book presents the key principles of lifecycle costing. The book concludes with a case study of a selection process, which proves illuminating as it contrasts the views of both contractors and professional advisors.

Chapter 2

Design and Build

Introduction

This chapter examines the principles and practice of Design and Build (D&B) procurement methods. As such, it provides the broader context for the detailed consideration of tendering in Chapter 3. To develop a realistic understanding of the use of D&B, the chapter draws on primary data collected from industry and a wide range of published material. This section commences by considering definitions of D&B before reflecting on the historical development and characteristics of the procurement method. The diversity of D&B types is then explored and presented in a continuum providing a clear typology. This enables important distinctions to be drawn. A major theme that was found to have an important influence on D&B projects was identified in the research data. The impact of using novation is explored in detail and provides the basis for the remainder of the chapter.

Design and Build defined

D&B procurement has been defined as follows.

> A building service where one organisation undertakes and accepts responsibility for both design and construction functions.
>
> (CIOB, 1988: p. vii)

The D&B approach is typically described as involving the client entering into an agreement with a single party, the principal contractor, who is assigned responsibility for the total project from the initial briefing through to final completion. However, as will be seen in this chapter, D&B can be considered a continuum that encompasses different levels of contractor involvement.

D&B differs markedly from traditional procurement, which can be defined as:

> the procedure whereby a client engages an architect and other consultants to design and control a building project and the construction is carried out by a main contractor appointed after competitive tender.
>
> (CIOB, 1988: p. viii)

Traditional contracting is characterised by the inherent fragmentation of the procurement process where the design is undertaken by one party, the architect, before being let to tender and then constructed by another party, the contractor.

The organisation and management structure for a D&B contract is shown in Figure 2.1. The functional role of the contractor embraces the management of the integrated design and construction process. This can be contrasted with the organisation and management structure for the traditional approach where the management and contractual relationships are separate, as shown in Figure 2.2.

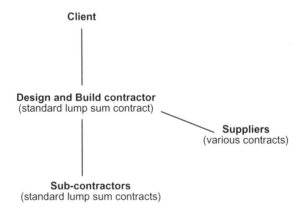

Figure 2.1. Management structure for a D&B contract indicating the functional role of the client and contractor (adapted from RICS (1996))

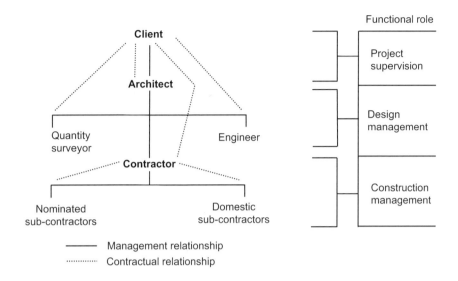

Figure 2.2. Management structure for a traditional contract indicating the functional roles of the parties (adapted from Griffith, 1989)

D&B can be considered as a 'family of procurement options', or variants, which are characterised by the contractor assuming greater responsibility for design and construction than with traditional contracting.

The historic origins of Design and Build

D&B, in concept, is far from being a new phenomenon. Before traditional procurement became dominant, many building projects were both conceived and built by the designer who engaged craftsmen to undertake the works. This was a practice steeped in history that was utilised until the early part of the twentieth century.

The traditional approach became popular at this time and was widely used until the late 1950s. At this time, a number of contractors began to offer the D&B Package Deal, so called because it offered clients a complete package of design and construction services. D&B can be said to have been rediscovered by contractors in response to traditional contracting, which was perceived to be problematic, often resulting in projects over budget, late and of poor quality.

The Emmerson report (1962) was an important catalyst for change in construction procurement, helping to initiate the shift from fragmented to integrated approach. Other influential reports and studies are considered in greater detail in Chapter 3.

Design and Build in practice

The Procurement Guide (RICS, 1996) states that the main advantages of a D&B approach are that:

- the client has only to deal with one firm
- inherent buildability is enhanced
- price certainty is obtained before construction starts, provided the client's requirements are adequately specified and changes are not introduced
- reduced total project time due to early completion is possible because of overlapping activities.

The Procurement Guide suggests that the disadvantages attendant to D&B are that:

- relatively fewer firms offer the D&B service so there is less real competition
- the client is required to commit himself before the detailed designs are completed
- in-house D&B firms are an entity so compensation for weak parts of the firm is not possible
- there is no design overview unless separate consultants are appointed by the client for this purpose
- difficulties can be experienced by clients in preparing an adequate brief
- bids are difficult to compare since each design, programme and cost will vary
- design liability is limited by the standard contract
- client changes to project scope can be expensive.

While a number of benefits of using D&B procurement are clearly suggested, what does design and build deliver in practice?

- Is project delivery speed faster?
- Is project cost reduced?
- Is better quality achieved?
- Is greater value for money obtained?

A landmark research report by Bennett *et al.* (1996) stated that 'our research shows that design-build is significantly better than traditional methods at delivering the greater certainty that comes from integrated systems' (p. 2). The main findings of this study are summarised below.

(*a*) Compared with traditional procurement, D&B exceeds construction speed by 12%, total project delivery speed by 30%, and cuts costs by 13%.

(*b*) Projects procured using D&B are 50% more likely to be completed on time, and more likely to be completed on budget.

(*c*) D&B is better at delivering projects on time when Employer's Requirements are minimal and the contractor is involved at an early stage in the design.

(*d*) There is greater cost certainty for D&B projects where Employer's Requirements are detailed, the worst performance on cost certainty is achieved with minimal Employer's Requirements development.

(*e*) The best performance in meeting clients' quality expectations is achieved where Employer's Requirements have minimal definition and where contractors' own in-house designers undertake design from an early stage.

(*f*) The worst outcome in meeting clients' quality requirements is where novation is used.

(*g*) Only 50% of D&B projects meet clients' expectations on quality, compared with a 60% satisfaction rate for traditional projects.

(*h*) D&B performs consistently better in meeting standards for complex or innovative buildings than for simple, standard, traditional buildings.

(*i*) Clients pay more to rectify defects in traditional contracting than in D&B.

Bennett *et al.* (1996) stated that customers consider that single point responsibility, guaranteed maximum cost and the minimisation of design and construction risks to be the significant factors for choosing D&B.

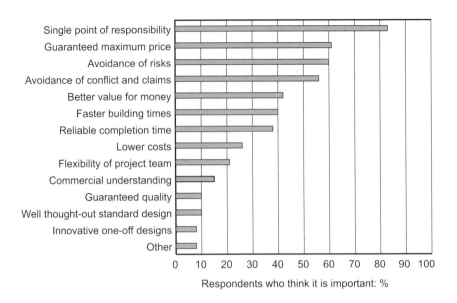

Figure 2.3. Why clients opt for design and build (adapted from Bennett et al., 1996)

When commissioning buildings, meeting functional needs, overall capital cost and aesthetics are important. Understanding the scope of the works, communication and the abilities of management staff are essential factors that were found to be important when selecting the project team. These key aspects are shown in Figures 2.3–2.5.

The Design and Build continuum

Various authors have conceptualised D&B in various ways. For example, Akintoye (1994) suggests that there are six types of D&B approach.

1. *Pure D&B*, sometimes called traditional D&B — where the contractor is fully responsible for the design and construction.
2. *Package deal* — where standardised, or system, buildings are altered to meet a client's particular requirements.

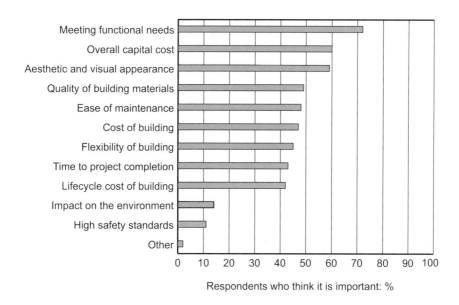

Figure 2.4. Clients' most important features when commissioning buildings (adapted from Bennett et al., 1996)

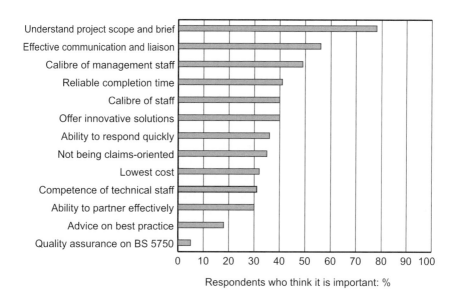

Figure 2.5. Clients' requirements for a D&B team (adapted from Bennett et al., 1996)

3. *Design and manage* — where the contractor is responsible for the design and supervision of sub-contractors although, unlike traditional, they are paid a management fee for their services.

4. *Design, manage and construct* — which is similar to design and manage but includes contractor involvement in the construction works.

5. *Novation* — where the client employs the services of a design consultant, who is then assigned to the contractor, following his appointment.

6. *Develop and construct* — where the client employs a design consultant to Stage 'D', or scheme design, of the Royal Institute of British Architects (RIBA) process and the contractor, when appointed, then completes the project by detailing and construction of the works.

In practice, many of these descriptions of D&B have become confused in application. For this reason, D&B procurement can be conceptualised as a *continuum* ranging from *pure D&B* to *detail-developed D&B*, which differ in the extent of design and specification development prior to contractor involvement. For example, a very prescriptive specification with well-developed drawings would represent a detail-developed form of approach, whereas a client who involves a contractor early in the process with minimal design having taken place would be using a pure D&B approach. With the latter, the design and specifications could be very well developed prior to awarding and agreeing the contract and commencing with site activities.

Many D&B approaches used today have been found to be *partially developed*, where the client and their consultants will have possibly developed the scheme to planning stage. This allows the contractors some scope for scheme development in their proposals, although this is controlled by the Employer's Requirements.

The increasing popularity of detail-developed D&B means that the potential benefits of integration and close working between client and contractor are lost. As D&B becomes more distant from pure D&B, many of the benefits of contractor involvement are reduced. The EPSRC study has found various reasons for the increasingly developed nature of D&B, which are shown below:

- risk
- tender cost and complexity
- project complexity and client type
- accelerated project programme

- consultant professionalism
- previous experience of contractors
- control issues
- integrated supply chains.

Risk

D&B is being used instead of traditional contracting, as it allows the client to transfer risk to the contractor. In this instance, clients are not choosing D&B for its integration benefits, but instead to avoid liability.

Tender cost and complexity

The classic D&B design competition, where contractors prepare different design proposals, is both costly to undertake and difficult to evaluate. Tender costs are generally higher than traditional contracting, and contractors ultimately need to recoup these through the industry. In addition, the often complicated nature of evaluating what can represent substantially different proposals leads clients to avoid using this type of D&B.

Project complexity and client type

Architects often advise clients to use developed D&B for complex schemes. This advice can be contrasted with the findings of Bennett *et al.* (1996) who found that D&B provided better quality than traditional contracting for complex and innovative schemes.

The status of the building client was found to be a major factor influencing the type of D&B being used. End users, who are generally more interested in the whole life of the building, tend to use more prescriptive specifications. However, attempting to maximise whole-life benefits by excluding contractor input until a late stage in the project is rather limiting, as it does not allow contractors to input their considerable experience in such issues.

Accelerated project programme

Clients often use D&B for its rapid time-frames. The need to fit site activities within very short time-frames leads clients to increase the amount of development work that is done before the contractor is involved. Instead of involving the contractor earlier through a two-stage or negotiated approach, clients often use detail-developed D&B in tandem with competitive tendering, thereby reducing contractor input.

Consultant professionalism

Many clients use developed D&B as they believe that consultants act more 'professionally' than contractors. Contractors and certain clients strongly opposed this view, drawing on specific examples. Clients need to consider that many contractors today are highly educated members of professional bodies and, hence, are required to work within ethical parameters.

Previous experience of contractors

Where clients have previously worked with contractors on purer D&B schemes and have not received a satisfactory building product, they sometimes develop the schemes further prior to allowing the contractor to become involved. This learned sensitivity can similarly be disseminated by architects who advise clients to develop the scheme to a well-defined stage prior to tender. There is a strong belief in the contracting and non-architect project-management community that architects favour for developed D&B is linked to their wish to reclaim their position as project leader.

Control issues

Clients wish to control the project for many different reasons. For example, they may be experienced and, therefore, have very firm ideas for scheme specification and design. Clients may require new developments to fit with existing developments, both from a maintenance and aesthetic perspective. Control of this type often results in very prescriptive specifications, which limit the contractor's ability to economically source products from the marketplace. Control can also stem from architects outsourcing design work, which then becomes specified in the tender documents. However, control can also stem from clients proactive purchasing policies. Integrating the 'supply chain' is one of the most popular new initiatives in construction management.

This buzzword needs a clear definition and Pearson (1999) believes it to mean:

- reducing the number of suppliers — reduces the bureaucracy
- working with suppliers earlier in the project — allows value addition and buildability aspects to be introduced.

The lack of diffusion and adoption of purchasing best practice (Robinson, 1997) can be seen beginning to be rectified by major companies in the UK. For example, one major contractor drew on outside expertise from the aerospace industry in selectively reducing the supply chain. This added value through design and management skills. In contrast, another contractor was more radical, reducing its list of suppliers from 28 000 to 7000 suppliers. Although such examples are associated with partnered approaches, EPSRC data suggest that some clients are developing their supply chains and moving these from project to project in conjunction with main contractor competitive tendering selection. This means that many of the specification, design and material choices are made prior to the scheme being competitively tendered. In this way, the integration of the supply chain is one reason for more developed D&B.

Many of the moves towards more detail-developed forms of D&B actively discourage the involvement of the contractor, and hence do not allow design and construction to be fully integrated. Much literature advises minimal pre-contractor scheme development, and promotes the contractor's early involvement in the scheme (CIOB, 1988; HM Treasury, 1999b; Hill, 2000; NAO, 2001). The benefits of early contractor involvement, such as buildability, constructability, economic sourcing and flexible programming, may encourage clients to readopt such practice. However, where clients have opted to develop an integrated supply chain in conjunction with competitively tendering the main contract, this simultaneously leads to more developed forms of D&B, although unlike many of the other reasons for adoption, this can potentially lead to many benefits for all concerned.

Novation in Design and Build

Novation is a legal term and, in a D&B context, its principal defining feature is that once the client's consultant has developed the project to tender stage and a contractor has been awarded the contract, the contractor then employs that same design consultant to complete the post-contract design stage. Novation is one derivative of D&B that can be conceived as a legal 'bolt on', and it applies to different types of consultants, including structural engineers, architects, and mechanical and electrical engineers. Novation has been confused with 'consultant switch' in the past. Chappell (1994), who states that the original contract between client and architect is rescinded with novation and a new one is established, differentiates the two legal concepts. Consultant switch involves the consultant being contractually bound to both the client and contractor, thus increasing the potential for a conflict of interest. Chevin (1993) understandably believes that the common usage of both terms can lead to confusion in practice.

Novation, as with other types of D&B, can facilitate buildability and constructability, with contractors working more closely with clients and designers (Griffith and Sidwell, 1995; CIIA, 1996). However, the potential benefits of novation have been viewed differently by consultants and contractors. Akintoye (1994) found that contractors generally view novation negatively as it 'does not put contractor's organisation in charge of the whole project but gives them the responsibility' (p. 162). Architects' perceptions of novation have been studied by Akintoye's later work with Fitzgerald (1995), where they discovered that architects unsurprisingly favour novation. The finding that architects favour novation is understandable when one considers that architects benefit from a secured revenue stream when it is used. It could be inferred that the clients' decision to adopt novation is being promoted by architects, as they are often the first point of contact for clients wishing to procure buildings.

Novation is clearly popular, Bennett *et al.* (1996) found that 37% of clients involved in their study used novation, and they believed it to be the fastest growing form of D&B. This popularity may be surprising when one considers that the same study attributed the worst performance in meeting customers' quality requirements to novation being used. This situation of high adoption and poor performance led the research team to examine the dynamics of novation from the principal contractor and architects perspective. This research uncovered seven main themes of enquiry; the majority highlighting the generally negative nature of novation:

- dual loyalties
- working at risk
- unrealistic programming

- drip-feeding of tender information
- value and risk issues
- contractor selection and team building
- advantages of novation.

Dual loyalties

Contractors stated that architects often continue to believe that they work for the client at post-contract stage when novation has taken place. In a similar way to the pre-contract short-circuiting that takes place, architects often continue to interact directly with the main project client despite contractors reinforcing the point that all communication should travel through themselves. Mosey (1998) and Siddiqui (1996) have previously highlighted this type of short-circuiting.

Such post-contract interaction can lead the architect to develop designs that did not form part of the tender proposal, possibly artificially increasing the client's expectations. Such practice is made possible by the architect's loyalties to the main project client, loyalty founded on the close contact at the initial stages of the project, the possibility of future work and the legacy of traditional contracting. Nevertheless, many architects interviewed did not believe that such fidelity was expected by clients at post-contract stage.

Working at risk

Many architects produce pre-contract information for clients on the basis that if the project goes ahead the architect will be novated to the contractor. However, this has been found to have wider negative consequences for the project, as shown below.

Tender information quality

The quality of the tender information produced can be compromised, as architects attempt to minimise the amount of work completed at risk. The study found that the quality of the information was so deficient in some instances that contractors had to employ engineers simply to allow them to price the project, despite the information having already been produced by a structural engineer prior to novation.

Relationship problems

Consultants' liquidity is often so low that they were found to have invoiced contractors who were still negotiating the contract award. Contractors stated that this seriously affected the early stages of their relationships with the novated consultant and, hence, had negative consequences for the project as a whole.

Continuous nature of working at risk

Consultants who have been novated are often still working at risk on other projects. Contractors complain that this reduces the quality of service that novated consultants provide. However, architects often state that they are forced to work at risk to secure work as clients often expect such a service.

Unrealistic programming

When the contractor has been selected, there is often a rush to start physical progress of the project on-site. As the consultants who have been novated have spent time at pre-contract stage familiarising themselves with the project, contractors expect them to be able to produce working drawings at short notice. However, consultants pointed out that contractors' demands for working drawings are often unrealistic. The fact that the consultants will often try to comply with these mandates can lead them to make poor decisions and release information that is incomplete.

Drip-feeding of tender information

Consultants pending novation are regularly contacted by contractors who are preparing their proposals as part of a tender competition. The number of requests means that the amount of time that can be given to every contractor is reduced. This results in information being slowly distributed, which places pressure on contractors trying to develop their proposals within the tender period. A surprising outcome of the drip-feeding of information is the contractors' desire for schemes to be developed further so that information is made available to them at tender stage. This is in contrast to contractors' typical views that the Employer's Requirements document should be relatively undeveloped and that the contractor should be allowed earlier and fuller input to the project.

Value and risk issues

Contractors are increasingly becoming skilled in value-oriented activities. Actively seeking to increase value for the client is increasingly being used to give contractors competitive advantage. Broadly speaking, such attempts to increase value require open communication between all parties involved. However, as the consultant pending novation interacts with all tendering contractors, the potential for competitive advantage being lost to other contractors is increased. Contractors recognise that consultants may communicate their ideas and, hence, this inhibits their value-engineering activities.

In addition, where the contractor does not have prior experience of the consultant, novation can affect the tender price as it represents a risk to the contractor. As with other such risks, the contractor allocates a price to them, thus potentially increasing the tender price.

Contractor selection and team building

Architects who have a close relationship to clients were found to be able to influence the selection of contractors. This was found mainly where architects were aware, either by experience or 'word of mouth', that a particular contractor did not pay consultants on time. In a situation where either the consultant–client relationship was not close enough to effect the client's decision, or the other benefits to the client outweighed the architect's views having any effect on selection, the consultant–contractor relationship was invariably found to be compromised.

Advantages of novation

Novation appears to lead to generally negative consequences for D&B. However, the study found that novation has some positive attributes, depending on whose perspective it is viewed from. The following factors were identified in the study.

Reduction in post-contract development

Contractors believe novation to be beneficial in respect to its ability to reduce the time needed for post-contract design development. As previously stated, this is viewed as a negative factor by the architects who are expected to produce drawings at short notice.

Learning curve

Contractors believe it to be beneficial that novation carries pre-contract design knowledge over to the post-contract phase. This allows the contractors clear access to the consultant's understanding of the client's needs. The importance of this factor increases as developed forms of D&B are used, as they isolate the contractor from the client.

The EPSRC study findings generally show novation to be disadvantageous. It creates a confusion of loyalties for the architect, various tender-related problems, and time pressures for tendering contractors. The general advice to clients is to use novation with caution, and consider the wider picture before adopting this approach.

Summary

D&B is a diverse continuum of procurement options which may be distinguished in a number of respects. Understanding the diverse characteristics of various D&B options is necessary before careful consideration can be given to appropriate tendering mechanisms. This chapter has outlined the development of D&B methods and has communicated current variants as a continuum ranging from pure D&B to detail-developed D&B. These extremes are distinguished based on the level of pre-contractor design and specification issues. The increasing popularity of more developed forms of D&B were explored along with the reasons behind these choices. A principle factor influencing the success of D&B projects was then considered in detail. Namely, the potential problems of using novation and the difficulties associated with design professionals working for the contractor.

Chapter 3

The development of tendering arrangements in the construction industry

Introduction

The aim of this chapter is to provide a framework for understanding the basic types of tendering practice used in the construction industry. This chapter is divided into two substantive areas. First, an overview of various reports that have considered, or influenced, UK tendering practice. Reflection on these publications helps to understand the development of trends in tendering and allows current practice to be contextualised. Several important themes emerge through the analysis, including: the importance of selective tendering; the development of pre-qualification procedures; and calls for more value-orientated selection. A basic understanding of the different approaches to tendering is then necessary before considering the specific problems associated with the evaluation of Design and Build (D&B) tenders. Hence, the second part of this chapter defines various types of tendering arrangements commonly used throughout the construction industry.

Evolution of tendering

To understand the evolution of tendering practice it is necessary to consider the major reports that have affected the industry. It will be shown that open tendering has been repeatedly criticised since the 1940s, while its replacement, selective tendering, has continually been promoted. Calls for the standardisation of pre-qualification exercises, and selection on the basis of overall value for money, were called for in the mid-1990s. More recent reports have focused on integrating the supply chain, and making costs and profit more transparent.

Simon Committee report (1944)

Tracing tendering history back to the days of the Second World War leads to the landmark Simon Committee report. Commissioned to examine the effectiveness of contemporary tendering procedures, the report focused on providing improvements to the placing and management of building contracts. This was at a time when large-scale construction investment in war-torn Britain was envisaged. The dominant tendering mechanism of the day, open tendering, was criticised for its lack of discrimination between contractors on any criteria other than capital cost. Additionally, open tendering was criticised for its inefficient use of contractors' resources, something which imposes inflationary pressure in the sector.

As an alternative to open tendering, the report promoted a selective approach, where contractors are first evaluated for performance potential prior to evaluation on the grounds of capital cost. Both open and selective tendering are considered in greater detail in later sections. As a catalyst for change from open to selective tendering, the report still affects current tendering practices where selective competition dominates. However, the new selective tendering mechanism was not a panacea; although it contained the logical framework for effective discriminatory selection, it was not at that time sufficiently developed to offer advanced selection processes. The principle of selecting the lowest capital cost tender is embodied in the NJCC code of practice for single-stage selective tendering (1996a) still being used in industry today. As will be discussed in further detail later, the decision to accept lowest cost is contrary to much current thought and, if practised, requires rigorous pre-qualification.

In addition to selective tendering, the Simon Committee promoted negotiation as a way to involve the contractor earlier in the project cycle, thus allowing the benefits of a more integrated team. The negotiated approach requires underpinning by reciprocal trust between parties to the building contract, something which this book suggests is often missing.

Banwell Committee report (1964)

Often cited, the Banwell report's central message promoting the benefits of integrated construction is still important today. The Banwell Committee firmly believed in the benefits of a cohesive project team, explicitly based on early contractor involvement, a practice that has still not been embraced by many factions of the building industry almost 40 years later. Their decision to promote this doctrine reflected the problems associated with the traditional contracting arrangement previously stated in Chapter 2. In addition to integrated teams, the committee argued that selective tendering should be more widely adopted, alternative approaches to contractor appointment should be utilised, and serial tenders should be promoted for their ability to allow ready formed teams the advantages of repetitive working.

Integrated project teams have since been adopted in various forms, for example, D&B, prime contracting, and management forms of procurement. Modern methods of contractor selection based on an integrated repeat-nature supply chain have, according to this study's research data and that of the popular construction press, been embraced. However, this adoption is often associated with large-scale experienced clients who have decided to commit resources to developing this essential early stage of the project cycle.

While clearly advocating the benefits of selective tendering, the report showed that 20 years after the Simon report, clients were firmly clinging to the economic free-market principle and utilising open tendering to fulfil their aim of securing the lowest cost. It was believed that open tendering also offered the most transparent method to ensure public accountability because it did not discriminate on grounds other than lowest capital cost. The fact that this was precisely the reason that the Simon Committee had criticised open tendering was not recognised by local authorities. Our data suggests that at almost 60 years post-Simon, local authorities are still struggling to appease what one respondent called 'the mythical auditor: champion of public accountability'.

Economic Development Committee for Building, *Action on the Banwell Report* (1967)

The Economic Development Committee for Building report followed shortly after the Banwell report and added voice to the criticism of open tendering. The report discovered that open tendering still found favour with government purchasing departments. For example, local authority housing, a department that had massive construction investment, was channelling investment through open tendering in 40% of instances. Hospital bodies, which were and still are large-scale clients of the construction industry, were using selective tendering, but sometimes using shortlists of as many as 12 contractors. This finding showed that the ability of selective tendering to reduce tendering costs and associated inflationary pressure was not being maximised at that time.

Constructing the Team, Sir Michael Latham (1994)

In the 1990s, Sir Michael Latham's landmark report embodied the need for change in an industry that had become defined by a claims conscious culture in the 1980s and early 1990s. Once more tolling the bell for selective tendering years after the early reports' message, the report focused on the integrity of the pre-qualification systems that underpin selective competition. Seizing on the need for a certificated system, it was argued that selection should be made on the basis of value for money and not lowest capital cost, as had previously been the ultimate decision factor.

A single pre-qualification document was seen as a way to reduce wastage and increase rigour in the selection process for all public-sector work. This, in turn, would lead to a single approved list, entry to which would be a prerequisite for tendering for public-sector work. Open tendering was again criticised for those who needed to hear this now somewhat antiquated advice. In addition to a central approved list, Latham advocated a reduction in the size of tender lists on D&B projects to three firms, in addition to advocating two-stage tendering for complex projects for which the D&B route was now being increasingly used.

Perhaps the two central themes running through all these major works was the move from open to selective tendering and the call to select contractors on the basis of value for money rather than simply lowest capital cost. While the above can broadly be considered one of *the* most influential reports of the last century, other tendering related publications are now considered.

Highlight Optimum Legitimate Tender (HOLT) technique (1995)

Although contained within numerous different publications, the HOLT technique as focused on here is drawn mainly from Holt's PhD thesis of

1995. This work is important in the academic field of tendering literature as it embraced multi-attribute decision-making explicitly in its development of a contractor selection model. Although multi-attribute analysis (MAA) has been considered in the past by many authors, the HOLT technique is useful as it shows in some detail how different decision criteria are developed and eventually matched to contractor attributes. His model, shown in Figure 3.1, is based on the following problems with tendering practice, which Holt identified through a literature review and survey.

1.   *Lack of universal approach* — tendering codes of practice are too broad to allow cohesive normalised tendering practice. Organisations rely on bespoke systems, the structure and detail of which are not shared with others for reasons of confidentiality. It is only when the systems fail that the organisation's belief in their integrity and effectiveness is questioned.

2.   *Long-term confidence in pre-qualification* — the confidence in pre-qualification is a function of the integrity of the design. Holt finds that the majority of pre-qualification systems are not very effective, a problem magnified by organisations' long-term confidence in them. For many contractors, pre-qualification leads to registration on a standing list, which, if not reviewed regularly, may not take account of organisations changing status in an often-volatile industry. In addition, many pre-qualification exercises do not take account of project-specific criteria.

3.   *Final selection and tender evaluation methods* — drawing on the relationship between lowest cost final selection and problematic projects as forwarded by other researchers in the field, Holt argues for a broader appraisal technique. Pointing to the civil engineering sector where qualified bids are the norm, the usefulness of the NJCC's advice to exclude qualified bids is questioned.

4.   *Subjective analysis* — tender evaluation often relies on subjective analysis. Although qualitative analysis is for Holt the lesser cousin to more quantitative techniques, he recognises the practical problems of following a purely quantitative approach; the cost of accruing the information, and the 'human factor' in analysis. In discussing the weighted techniques that are utilised in many authors' tender selection techniques, Holt argues that objective output is based on subjective input.

Holt's main aim is increasing the rigour and quality of the pre-qualification process while simultaneously grouping all processes;

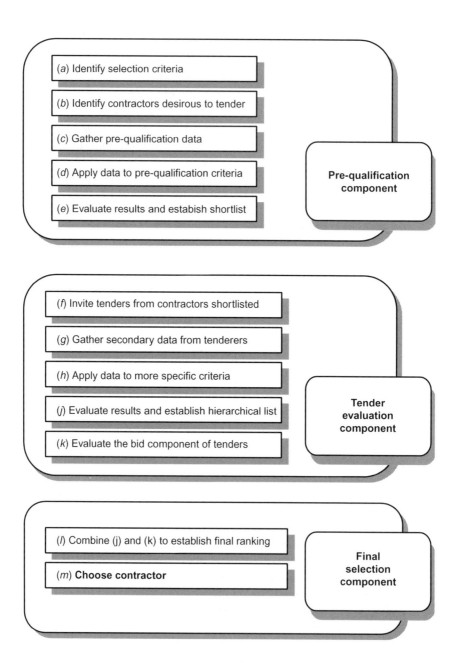

Figure 3.1. Framework for the stepwise logic model (adapted from Holt, 1995)

general qualification, project-specific qualification and final tender assessment within one model. However, the model depends on certain mathematical principles, which practitioners may neither be familiar with nor have the time to become acquainted with. For this reason, the model should not be used without a thorough understanding, otherwise 'black box' syndrome could result. Holt's work on developing criteria and evaluating contractor attributes is particularly illuminating and is drawn on within this book. Despite being focused on pre-qualification and tender assessment for traditional contracts, many facets are able to be utilised in D&B contractor selection.

Construction Industry Board, *Code of Practice for the Selection of Main Contractors* (1997)

In contrast to some of the previously discussed publications, the Construction Industry Board (CIB) guide was not intended as a forum for industry change, but as a practical document. The guide is deliberately broad in highlighting elements of best practice in the selection of main contractors. Its objectives are improving efficiency, reducing duplication and wastage in tendering, while simultaneously facilitating an increase in client satisfaction.

Whereas Holt (1995) details many assessment criteria and sub-criteria, and deals in detail with each one, the CIB publication outlines 10 initial qualification criteria. There are differing views regarding whether guides should offer prescriptive or broader-based advice. Holt develops a specific model with well-defined criteria forming an essential element, yet the CIB document differs as it is a more generic document, providing less prescriptive signposts to best practice.

The qualification process, similar to Holt's, begins with non-project specific criteria, before moving on to consider project-specific criteria and final assessment. Following previous reports, the CIB guide advocates short tender lists, although when discussing D&B projects offers no actual differentiation between the types of D&B project that this book has found to be so crucial.

The CIB's main aim in producing the guide is to forward the following notions of good practice.

1. Clear procedures — which allow fairness and transparency.
2. Tender lists should be compiled systematically from qualified contractors.
3. Tender lists should be as short as possible.

4. Equity for tenderers — all tenderers should be assessed under the same conditions.
5. Confidentiality — tenderers' confidentiality should be respected at all times.
6. Time — sufficient time should be scheduled for the preparation and evaluation of tenders.
7. Quality and price — tenders should be evaluated under both these criteria.
8. Collusion — practice should be directed to avoid collusion.

Construction Industry Research and Information Association, *Selecting Contractors by Value* (1998)

The Construction Industry Research and Information Association (CIRIA) best practice guide is concerned primarily with selecting the project team based on their ability to add value. Following the value for money message embedded in the Latham report, a clear definition of the client's value system is the starting point for the approach. In contrast to the value for money rhetoric evident in many reports and industry sound bites, the CIRIA guide provides an accomplished account of selecting contractors on the basis of value input. The guide describes eight selection criteria, with associated sub-criteria as follows.

1. Technical knowledge and skills.
2. Management skills — time, cost, value, quality, risk, health and safety, impact on the environment.
3. Effective internal organisation.
4. Collaborative culture.
5. Appropriate human resources.
6. Supply chain management.
7. Financial resources.
8. Broad indicators.

Rethinking Construction, The Report of the Construction Industry Task Force, Sir John Egan (1998)

Also commonly referred to as the Egan report, this government-initiated industry reform report was similar to the *Constructing the Team* report of 1994, and it extended its predecessor's potential impact for efficiency savings through directly adopting manufacturing techniques. Setting optimistic targets for industry productivity improvements and for the reduction of waste and defects, the report led to the formation of different bodies to implement its initiatives. The sequential nature of the construction process was highlighted as a barrier to utilising the skills and knowledge of suppliers and constructors. Focus was also directed at the typical process of selecting a new project team of designers, suppliers and constructors for the project. The commonly applied selection procedures were, it was argued, inhibiting learning, innovation and the overall development of the team. These principles have been adopted by many large-scale organisations and are driving long-term supply chain initiatives.

Various best practice bodies are currently operating as part of the rethinking construction initiative. These include the following:

- Movement for Innovation (M4I)
- Construction Best Practice Programme (CBPP)
- The Housing Forum
- The local government task force
- Respect for People
- IT Construction Best Practice
- Centre for Construction Innovation (CCI)
- Design Build Foundation (DBF).

The authors consider it vital that readers contact relevant organisations, including those in the above list, and actively become involved with them. For example, the CBPP runs a programme to identify, implement and sustain best practice by focusing on the following activities.

1. Encourage early interest in best practice.
2. Facilitate more involvement in best practice.
3. Develop and maintain leaders in best practice.

Various initiatives are currently operational including the Construction Best Practice Club programme. This allows all sizes and disciplines of construction business to learn and improve from each other. Involvement with this type of initiative has been found to be extremely beneficial to those involved.

Having presented major works outlining the historic development of construction tendering it is now necessary to define the various tendering arrangements.

Tendering arrangements in the construction industry

Open tendering

Open tendering closely embraces free-market competition as it does not limit the amount of organisations who are allowed to tender for construction schemes. The simple logic that underpins open tendering is that an increase in competition leads to a reduction in costs. Additionally, the client need not get involved in the time-consuming process of pre-qualifying contractors for performance potential. However, as discussed later, this tendering mechanism may be associated with a waste of contractors' resources leading to price inflation, in addition to claims-active practices aimed at reversing unprofitable bids. Notwithstanding, open tendering is still used widely in other industries and contains the following elements.

1.   Advertisement showing project particulars, requesting contractors to apply for the full tender documents.
2.   Tender documents are released typically after the deposit of funds by interested contractors.
3.   Contractors submit their bid and are typically selected on the basis of lowest capital cost.

Although open tendering has, upon occasion, been discredited in the UK following continued criticism in industry transformation reports, a relatively recent report (Holt *et al.*, 1996) has suggested that it is making a surprising return to favour. The EPSRC research study found that clients still used open tendering in 6·1% of occasions, a relatively low figure yet still interesting based on the arrangement's limitations. Baker and Osraah's (1985) study found that 14·9% of clients used open competition. Despite offering accountability benefits, as its only distinguishing criteria is cost, the mechanism can be considered antiquated and its use may well result in the client regretting their decision. In the United States, open tendering is referred to as the 'low-bid method' and was embraced by the public sector until popular opinion suggested that the electorate were no longer getting the best value for money. Low-bid is principally supported in the US for the way that objective selection based on price secures against corruption and improper practice, in addition to offering low costs. Herbsman and Ellis (1992) state that its disadvantages are that:

- quality and time issues are not allowed a place in evaluation
- bid-rigging can take place
- unreasonably low bids are prevalent.

As in the UK, such methods are now decreasing in popularity and use, following increased awareness and research and development in the field of construction procurement.

Selective tendering

Selective tendering is fundamentally different to open tendering as it seeks to limit the number of contractors able to tender. It does this by employing a pre-qualification process to select contractors that meet or exceed predetermined criteria. Pre-qualification is dealt with later in this section, although, as its name suggests, it requires tenderers to be qualified prior to being allowed to tender. Selection criteria are both general and project specific, and seek to reduce the possibility of awarding a contract to a contractor who cannot perform within the necessary client performance thresholds. Successful pre-qualification will either allow a contractor to bid on an individual project or on a range of potential projects, depending on the approach implemented by the client and the individual mechanisms employed to procure their projects. The disadvantages of selective tendering are:

- the time and resources required to conduct the evaluation process and keep up-to-date approved lists
- that competitiveness is decreased in proportion to the size of the tender list
- that accountability could be considered harder to demonstrate than with open tendering, as marking subjective qualification criteria is open to interpretation
- that the criteria used in selection may not be sufficiently well developed or may not be tailored to the specific needs of the project.

The qualification criteria can be developed in-house by the client or his consultants, and could be based on experience, reference to academic research or industry reports, or simply by following/adapting codes of practice. Selective tendering is embodied in the JCT *Practice Note Six* (2002), and National Joint Consultative Committee (NJCC, 1995; 1996a; 1996b) documents, which are still used in industry today despite the committee no longer being operational.

Selective tendering is further categorised as either single stage or two stage, and the NJCC provide documents for both alternatives. It is important to consider single- and two-stage mechanisms in relation to the NJCC documentation, as these codes of procedure form the basis of much tender practice in the UK.

Single-stage selective tendering

Essentially, the client will develop a tender list of contractors — the shortlist — from his own longlist or a stand-alone pre-qualification process and then in the majority of instances evaluate contractors' bids on lowest capital cost. The longlist can be drawn up in various ways, including national registers, contacting trade bodies and professional institutions or by directly placing adverts. The tender list is developed through application of pre-qualification criteria to potential contractors. The NJCC (1996a) presupposes that the quality of contractors is dealt with adequately by the pre-qualification process. Following a yes/no binary pre-qualification decision, evaluation on lowest capital cost is sufficient. As will be seen, this dictum is the opposite of that currently called for within the industry, although research data show it is often the overriding principle applied. This process is simple in essence, and the NJCC believed it to be suitable in a majority of instances. Its favour is represented in the EPSRC study findings, which show that 48·5% of clients still use single-stage selective tendering. This is similar to the 40·4% usage reported in Baker and Osraah (1985).

Two-stage selective tendering

Two-stage tendering is advocated for use in 'large or complex projects where close collaboration with the contractor during the design stage will assist the search for the best solution for the employer in terms of cost, programme and design' by JCT *Practice Note Six* (2002: p. 12). When one takes into account the importance that early involvement is given in the majority of industry best-practice advice, it is surprising that surveys continually indicate relatively low-adoption rates for two-stage tendering. Data obtained in the EPSRC study showed that 15·2% of clients indicated they used this approach in most circumstances. The NJCC produces two-stage tendering documents for traditional contracting arrangements (NJCC, 1996b) in addition to including two-stage tendering for D&B projects (NJCC, 1995), which is discussed subsequently.

Two-stage tendering encompasses a variety of various approaches, but all follow the same basic sequence and include an element of negotiation. The first stage involves some element of competition, for example, pricing preliminaries, overheads or a schedule of rates based on initial designs. Following the first stage, no contract has been agreed between contractor and client. These rates are then used in the second stage, to negotiate the tender sum, as the scheme is developed. The major difference between single stage and two stage is that with two stage the contractor is involved in developing the project design. The NJCC code advises that a maximum of six contractors be included on the first-stage tender list following pre-qualification. This number should be reduced to four if there is sufficient developmental work required by the contractor to submit the first-stage bid, although in practice it may not operate in this way.

It should be pointed out that the precise differentiation between single- and two-stage tendering aids explanation, yet ultimately some overlap occurs. The JCT *Practice Note Six* states that:

> there are many 'single stage' projects which in terms of particular detail inevitably involve an element of second stage discussion and negotiation. However, where a single stage procedure is adopted, it is essential that the discussion and negotiation of residual issues should not be such as in any way to undermine the integrity of the process
>
> (JCT, 2002: p. 12)

Serial tendering

Serial tendering essentially relates to projects of a similar nature, or a staged production of a scheme where the client can benefit from repetition and standardisation. It is an agreement that the initial tender on one scheme provides the basis of follow-on projects under the same conditions that characterise this type of tender arrangement. Fluctuations for inflation are associated with this type of arrangement, as the contracts may run over large time-frames. Efficiency savings may be incorporated into the document, possibly in the form of target cost-arrangements in addition to awarding further work on satisfactory performance reviews.

Fully negotiated approaches

This type of tender mechanism is typically used in situations where the client has previous successful experience with a contractor. Although sometimes associated by some with slightly higher costs, research suggests the approach is increasingly finding favour as it allows early contractor involvement in the project, better team relationships and more of a cohesive problem-solving attitude. In addition, the actual outturn costs may ultimately be lower with negotiation, as it allows all parties to gain a deeper understanding of the scheme thereby allowing more realistic planning to be undertaken. Negotiation was used by 18·2% of clients sampled during the EPSRC study, while partnering was categorised separately and accounted for 12·1% of clients' use. Associated with D&B projects, the approach can vary widely from single-project negotiation to framework-type agreements for numerous projects. Many approaches that were encountered in the study used a quantity surveyor to represent the client, providing an external auditing and cost-development function. In D&B projects, this approach is often used by developer–clients, and the data provide numerous examples of satisfied clients and contractors using this approach. The study found that when contractors are involved in negotiated projects, they are more likely to select sub-contractors for their performance rather than their cost. For example, a contractor stated:

> 'I mean on negotiated don't get me wrong, in negotiated work the only difference normally tends to be you won't trawl the market quite so deeply with the sub-contractors that you are looking to tender for you. We would tend to include people in our bid who we know absolute 100% are going to do a fine job for us.'

Many participants considered the above view to be completely alien to them, as it suggests a lack of client care and pride in the product.

Taking into account the fact that negotiation is often used where client and contractor have previously worked together, the research data suggest that project-specific qualification and financial review are sometimes not undertaken. With respect to financial reviews, this element should always be considered necessary, irrespective of previous experience, such is the potential for a contractor's stability to change in a short space of time, and the need for parity between tendering contractors. Hatush and Skitmore (1997) state that financial status is measured by the following decision parameters: credit status, bank status, bond status and the published accounts report. Readers are referred to this work for further reading. Project-specific criteria should also be revisited where the scheme differs in respect to previous examples. The disadvantages of negotiation that were found to hinder adoption include the following.

1.   Cost is perceived to be higher than in competition. A consensus figure of 2–3% higher costs were identified by the data. Ashworth (1996) believes the figure to be in the order of 5%. However, as mentioned, the outturn costs could actually be lower in addition to the other benefits that negotiation can deliver, such as better programming.

2.   The perception that it is difficult to provide accountability — a problem not limited to the public sector. It should be noted that open-book accounting techniques and the use of independent professional consultants do allow accountability to be demonstrated.

3.   Clients sometimes perceive a general lack of financial control when negotiating with contractors. Some clients can occasionally feel that they have no control over the costs. They feel that they are at the mercy of contractors, although this is reduced by a close relationship with the consultant quantity surveyor. The perception needs tempering with the fact that cost certainty is present at a later stage, where a detailed cost plan is used. Some employers' agents argued that open-book accounting is never truly open book as they believe that contractors keep two books, one for clients and one for themselves which holds the true picture. A fully audited approach is required to dispel these problems; in addition the nature of the contracting organisation is key, with many contractors interviewed heavily defending their open conduct in negotiated approaches.

Summary

This chapter commenced by providing an overview of various publications concerned with tendering. Several themes emerged from this chronological analysis, including the importance of pre-qualification and selective tendering. However, the overarching argument can be summarised as a call for better value in the procurement of construction. The second part of the chapter was used to define popular forms of tendering currently used in today's construction industry. These principles are then developed in more detail in later chapters when the specifics of D&B tender evaluation are considered.

Chapter 4

Pre-qualification

Introduction

The pre-qualification process associated with tendering has consistently emerged in both primary data and industry reports as a critical factor in the overall success of projects. The aim of this chapter is to explore the goals of pre-qualification and examine various issues surrounding the process. For example, assessing pre-qualification criteria, the preliminary enquiry, practical applications, and the use of interviews and presentations are discussed. The use of pre-qualification outside the UK construction industry is then considered as an aid to best practice. Finally, the chapter concludes with a previously published model of pre-qualification.

Pre-qualification explained

Pre-qualification is the essential component of selective tendering. It is the process by which contractors are assessed for their potential to complete the scheme in a competent manner, meeting the performance demands set by the client. Russell (1996) defines the process as one where 'an owner, or a team of qualified individuals whom the owner designates for the task, screens the candidate contractors according to a given set of criteria *before* any competitive bidding or price negotiation occurs. The goal of this screening process is to determine a constructor's competence and capabilities to perform the work if the owner awards the organisation the contract' (pp. 1–2). Russell sees pre-qualification as a filter process and this is a useful metaphor; the essential elements being the construction and application of the different criteria providing the filter process. It should be noted that the terms pre-qualification, selection and award process are sometimes used in different ways. For example, the HM Treasury (1999a) terms the pre-qualification process the selection process, while the tender invitation, evaluation, contract award and debrief are termed the award process.

Pre- and post-qualification

Qualification can be conducted prior to evaluating the contractor's tender (pre-qualification), or following evaluation of the contractor's tender (post-qualification). Post-qualification in isolation is sometimes associated with open tendering, and as such is not advocated. However, in many instances post-qualification often follows pre-qualification where the criteria are revisited to aid in final selection.

Pre-qualification can be conducted on two levels using either:

- *general criteria* — leading to registration on an approved list, or the initial part of a pre-qualification process, or
- *project-specific criteria* — developed in relation to the actual project, the results of which are used to determine the actual tender list.

The advent of selective tendering has meant that clients, often with the help of their advisors, need to conduct pre-qualification exercises. It has been found over the years by various authors that the quality of pre-qualification process utilised often leaves a lot to be desired. Russell (1996) found the following problems with pre-qualification.

1. It is not as effective as most people think.
2. Clients fail to ask for relevant information.
3. When they do collect the correct information, those evaluating it often do not know how to relate it to the probability of failure.

This last point underlines Russell's focus in studying pre-qualification; identifying potential for failure. Many contractors interviewed saw the pre-qualification process as being aimed at disqualifying poor contractors, rather than pre-qualifying capable contractors. The concentration on avoiding the negative consequences of appointing an inappropriate contractor, characterises the general nature of pre-qualification in the US. A typical approach in the US involves a surety bond company conducting the pre-qualification process. These companies are, as their name suggests, financial in nature, and generally not well versed in construction-specific issues. This often translates into a narrow financial focus on the pre-qualification of contractors. In this type of approach, an external body not directly tied into the client's project-team conducts the process. This ultimately distances the client from the process, thus minimising the ability to foster early team relationship building and project familiarity. This rather obvious disadvantage is important when one considers that the early formation of relationships helps to reduce disputes and conflicts (Russell, 1996).

Luckily perhaps, surety bond companies, and their execution of the pre-qualification process, need not concern UK clients and practitioners, thus negating this potentially problematic factor. Instead, the client has every opportunity to be involved in the process, allowing it to more adequately reflect the ultimate objectives for the project. This book does not consider individual criteria in any great depth, instead concentrating on an outline of pre-qualification and its relationship to the wider selection process. Following consideration of the main issues involved, readers should be able to develop a pragmatic approach. According to the Construction Industry Development Agency of Australia (CIDA, 1995), their pre-qualification process offers five key advantages, as follows.

1. It brings greater objectivity into the decision-making process by optimising predictability.
2. It requires evidence of management systems, rather than rigid standards or ratios.
3. It encourages self-assessment and objective setting to achieve world-class best practice in increasing industry capability.
4. It is a tool to assess financial and technical risk.
5. It provides contractors with a consistent basis to tender and negotiate.

Developing a pre-qualification system requires the client to decide on the following attributes of the system.

1. Develop a clear prioritised list of project objectives, which could be linked to a formal value-management process.
2. Operationalise the above into criteria related to contractor attributes that can be clearly measured.
3. Weight the above criteria relative to the client's project objectives.

4. Develop and clearly indicate the detail and extent of information required from bidders, taking account of the cost of information and its usefulness.

Various approaches can be adopted. For example, the study found that in many instances experienced clients have developed a bespoke pre-qualification system, while inexperienced clients may often make use of external consultants who will have experience in these practices. Whichever type of approach is adopted, it is beneficial if the client has input into the pre-qualification process. Where the client is procuring a singular discrete project, the generic and project-specific pre-qualification factors can be undertaken in one exercise.

Assessing pre-qualification criteria

General and project-specific criteria need developing. Consideration needs to be given to how to assess contractors' attributes in relation to the selection criteria. Thought should be given to the usefulness of criteria, with each criterion and sub-criterion needing to earn its place in the evaluation, otherwise wasteful and ineffective practices be adopted. The amount of effort required in providing the information should be borne in mind:

- will contractors have the information to hand?
- will much time and effort be required to provide the information in the form required?
- is there the possibility that certain data elements can be electronically supplied and analysed?
- consider the usefulness of updating information that has previously been supplied by contractors — a more selective approach may prove more efficient.

This research study finds that pre-qualification is often viewed with disdain by contractors, for example in response to the question, *Is pre-qualification a rigorous process, and do you think it is worthwhile?*, a contractor with years of experience in D&B answered:

'Nine times out of ten they are just going through the process, I think they already know, I mean the client relies on the consultants as to who should be on the list because they don't really know. The consultants, surveyors, they know the contractors that have done that particular type of job, although there might be 12 on the list to be pre-qualified they know which six will be on the final six or four and I think it is just a paper exercise.'

This statement not only shows the contractor's belief in the lack of the usefulness of pre-qualification, but also the way it is grounded in the belief that consultants having predetermined who will be included in the tender list. This negative view of pre-qualification is not shared by consultants, for whom it is often considered to be a key element of the selection process. However, sceptical contractors link consultants' enthusiasm to its fee-earning potential.

Contractors' often negative views of pre-qualification grow to some extent in relation to the size and bureaucratic nature of the process. Local authorities were singled out for criticism, as they often require contractors to complete lengthy questionnaires requiring the same information from project to project. Much of the information is seen as superfluous by contractors, as one makes clear:

'I think a lot of the time they are paying lip service to the pre-qualification concept, I mean, I'll cite an example for a local authority. Every job that's coming out of this local authority we get the same questionnaire to answer and the questionnaires are 30, 40 pages long for us to go through.'

It seems that it is the perception of a lack of relevance and the amount of time and resources required to complete the requisite information that is the problem; rigorous pre-qualification can, at times, become overdemanding. Data show that contractors' lack of enthusiasm for pre-qualification sometimes fails to take account of the importance that certain information is kept up to date. The case for recent reliable financial data has previously been discussed. However, some contractors do not recognise its importance, possibly because of their own organisational stability. The following quote, taken from an interview with a surveyor in a contracting organisation, shows this clearly:

'. . . to be given questionnaire after questionnaire for pre-qualification makes you think does it matter how many years we have been with our bank'.

Clearly, such things do matter in the economically volatile world of construction. Contractors interviewed highlighted a paradox of producing financial information. This paradox involves the client expecting the contractor's financial background to be made available in some detail, yet when contractors requested the same assurances of the client's financial background prior to undertaking scheme development work, the clients often took offence and often refused to provide such information. There is clearly a need for a reciprocal relationship with regard to such information.

An effective pre-qualification need not be an overdemanding process. The calls for standardisation of the pre-qualification process as, for example, in Holt's work and that of Latham are important in this area as they allow the information to be collated and produced efficiently. Standardisation need not stop the customisation of criteria to take into account the particular project and client. Typically, much of the information requested from contractors will be similar from project to project and, as such, most contractors will keep this to hand and modify it in relation to each project.

One consistent theme that was encountered in the study was the importance given to contractors' previous experience on similar projects. It is generally accepted that contractors and their consultants who wish to be involved in D&B projects should ideally have experience of using this procurement route. As stated previously, many D&B schemes tendered today are effectively risk-transferred conventional contracts. The client needs to be aware of the different types of D&B that the contractor has worked on in the recent past. Knowledge of this can be used to match experience and ability with the nature of the proposed scheme. Knowledge that the contractor has been involved with successful negotiated approaches with clients, may indicate the contractor's ability and willingness to input into the project. This can often lead to advantages, including alternatives being offered both at the tender stage and during the actual construction phase. Ideally, the contractor and client will interact closely during the project, the success of which depends to a large degree on personal relationships. This, and other issues, are often best dealt with during an interview session.

Problems where pre-qualification is not used

Potter and Sanvido (1994) discuss a scheme procured using D&B. The client, the US Army Corps of Engineers, were relatively new to D&B and, as such, allowed 16 organisations to submit bids. The scheme, a $58·4 million centre for missile excellence, was procured in such a way that 15 contractors had to absorb the wasted cost of preparing a significant D&B tender submission. Ultimately, these costs are passed on to the subsequent clients of the contractor. It is perhaps these initial problems that have led the US Army Corps of Engineers to develop very prescriptive detailed selection procedures. In addition to limiting resource wastage, a lack of pre-qualification can lead to unsuitable bidders being selected, itself often related to a multitude of negative consequences.

Practicalities of pre-qualification

Pre-qualification factors should be developed by taking account of general and project-specific factors. The NJCC D&B tender code (1995) suggests the following issues should be considered:

- the firm's financial standing and record
- whether the firm has had recent experience of designing and constructing the type of building envisaged by the Employer's Requirements under conditions similar to those detailed by the employer
- whether the contractor's customary design capability is in-house and, if not, what method will be used in order to provide a design capability
- the firm's general experience and reputation in the area in question
- whether the management structure of the firm is adequate for the type of contract envisaged, and
- whether the firm will have adequate capacity at the relevant time.

A longlist of contractors needs developing from the client's previous experience, advertising the scheme, for example with Official Journal of the European Communities (OJEC) regulations, or from consultant experience. This longlist needs to be reduced to a shortlist of contractors who will be able to tender for the project.

Nine pre-qualification criteria are utilised in the example shown in Figure 4.1, adapted from Wong *et al.* (1999). The project-specific criteria are based on a study of clients' preferred project-specific pre-qualification criteria. This pre-qualification list is intended as a brief outline. To aid clarity and understanding, a 10-point scoring scale is shown above. However, there is debate over the perception of accuracy that different scales give. For example, CIRIA (1998) advises the use of a four-point

Project-specific criteria and sub-criteria	Weighted score	Score	Lowest total score
Manpower resources Quality and quantity of human resources Quality and quantity of managerial staff Amount of decision-making authority on site Amount of key personnel for the project			
Equipment resources Type of plants and equipment available Size of equipment available Condition and availability of equipment Suitability of the equipment			
Project-management capabilities Number of professional personnel available Type of project control and monitoring procedures Availability of project-management software Cost control and reporting systems Ability to deal with unanticipated problems			
Geographical familiarities Contractor's familiarity with weather conditions Contractor's familiarity with local labour Contractor's familiarity with local suppliers Contractor's familiarity with geographic area Relationship with local authority			
Location of home office Home office location relative to job site location Communication and transportation – office to job site			
Capacity Current workload Maximum resource/financial capacity Finance arrangements			
Project execution to the proposed project Training or skill level of craftsmen Productivity improvement procedures and awareness Site organisation, rules and policies (health and safety) Engineering coordination			
Technical-economic analysis Comparison of client's estimate with tender price Comparison between proposal and average tender prices Comparison for client's and proposed direct cost Contractor's errors – proposed construction method, etc. Proposals review – cost/time/resources schedule			
Other project-specific criteria Actual quality achieved to the similar works Experience with specific type of facility Proposed construction method Ability to complete on time Actual schedule achieved on similar works			

Figure 4.1. Pre-qualification criteria (adapted from Wong et al.,1999)

scale ranging from -1 to +2, as they believe a 10-point scale gives a spurious impression of accuracy. Other approaches to scaling concepts can be used, for example the methods used in describing risk include Likert scales, textual and colour bandings.

Preliminary enquiry

Following development of the longlist, the client needs to provide the contractors with information about the scheme, both to assess their suitability through the pre-qualification exercise and also to allow the contractor to assess whether they wish to bid. Janssens conceptualises two types of D&B tender enquiry — the orthodox and unorthodox enquiry. These issues are outlined below, but for a more comprehensive explanation refer to the original book (Janssens, 1991).

Orthodox enquiry

This is 'professionally' assembled and contains typical information, such as the tender period, contract terms and conditions, and a clear brief. With this type of tender, the contractor can decide to either tender or decline to tender.

Unorthodox enquiry

This type of request for proposals is not well structured, the terms and conditions are not made explicit, the tender period is not provided, and it generally appears rather vague. Jannsens outlines five decisions that the contractor can make with this type of tender.

1. Decline to develop any proposals altogether.
2. Decline to develop any proposals, but quote fees.
3. Submit a budget costing without developing proposals.
4. Submit a budget costing and develop proposals.
5. Submit a full firm-price tender and develop proposals.

The contractor's decision to progress from point 1 to point 5 will be based on various issues, such as the following.

1. The probability of the project proceeding.
2. The probability that the contractor will secure the contract.
3. The potential profitability.
4. The risk factors involved.
5. The organisational resources available to develop the bid.
6. The resources available to develop the design and to construct the project.
7. The relationship with the client and consultants.
8. The probability of future work.

Although unorthodox enquiries may be rare in other forms of procurement, such as traditional contracting, in some respects they suit the conventional understanding of D&B as a direct union of contractor and client. The EPSRC study data show that unorthodox enquiries are associated with pure D&B, and often in conjunction with negotiation. The following response given in an interview with a contractor is illuminating:

'Only about 5% of the D&B that we do is like that, we've got some super examples of it whereby on one job the client came directly to us, we appointed an architect to work for us and an engineer to work for us, he's had a QS [quantity surveyor] look over our shoulder at the figures, but essentially we went and got planning, we got building reg's approval, and negotiated a price with him from there, so that's D&B in its absolute ultimate blank sheet of paper, "I want a water bottling factory" was the brief and that was it, and that's true D&B for me, it will be a very successful job because we had been involved from day one, the client knows exactly when he can have his building in terms of programme, he knows exactly what he is getting because the dialogue has been over the table with him directly and not through an employer's agent and that will be a highly successful job, it has been so far and it will just continue in the same vain.'

Where the client opts to utilise an orthodox enquiry, the JCT *Practice Note Six* (2002) provides a model form of preliminary enquiry letter in addition to a project information schedule and questionnaire. The project information schedule outlines the details of the project and allows contractors to make a decision on their willingness to tender. The NJCC D&B code of procedure (1995) states that a D&B preliminary enquiry letter should include the following:

- site survey, including boundaries
- party walls and adjoining buildings
- trial pit or borehole information

- survey of existing services and obstructions
- information on mains services supply and outfall availability
- wayleaves and restrictive covenants
- ownership and other legal issues
- statutory permissions obtained, including conditions
- statutory permissions required
- building insurance, scope and payment
- special risks and special risk insurance
- design warranties
- collateral warranties
- user requirements, written and drawn information
- performance specification
- specific building materials required
- fitting out requirements
- employer-designed components
- occupation prior to completion or stage completions
- testing requirements
- building maintenance requirements
- latent defect insurance, parties and duration
- any other special requirements.

The questionnaire sent as part of the preliminary enquiry elicits pre-qualification information, and should be augmented with a pre-qualification interview. Although the contractor will typically not have begun any proposal development at this early stage, it gives all parties an opportunity to discuss the scheme, including clarifying specific issues, and giving the contractor an opportunity to access the client and gain valuable experience of their project objectives.

Interviews and presentations

A recurring theme in this book is the importance of the presentation and interview to the selection of the contractor. Presentation and interview allows both sides to gain a greater understanding of each other and to communicate in a dynamic environment. However, whether this takes place as part of the pre-qualification process or as part of the communication of the Contractor's Proposals, there is the feeling that it is the presentation skills, rather than the product, both organisation and construction, that is taken into account. A contractor summates his thoughts on this issue:

'I think in a lot of instances it's down to the personality that actually gets sent to the pre-tender interviews, because I think that is basically the crux of it. You send out all the questionnaires they want, you put all the answers down that you feel are going to get you on to that list, but at the end of the day it's the people that you send down to see these people that's going to dictate whether or not you get on the tender list.'

The perception of presentations as superficial is similarly shared by consultants, who recognise that good presentation skills do not always relate to appropriate selection, as a senior architect comments:

'You're always looking for value for money, how much you can glean from someone who is trying to sell you their firm and whether they are going to do that is questionable. Its having the right people I think, its making the right noises to tell you the truth, if you come across well at interview, you can be a load of rubbish at building, but you've probably got on the tender list.'

The contractor's recognition that he or she is a part player in a somewhat superficial game of appearances and perception creation is often regarded negatively by contractors. The problem stems from the high-level staff that are involved in interviews and presentations, and the corresponding high staffing costs. Presentations can sometimes involve three to four staff from the contractor's organisation on the presentation day, in addition to the preparation time required. This expense is undertaken at risk for the contractor and, as such, needs to be taken into account in the decision to tender.

A clear piece of advice to clients is to ideally ensure that the team providing the tendering organisation's presentation includes some members of staff who would actually be involved in the day-to-day running of the project. It is often the case that where this does not take place, clients can sometimes feel slightly beguiled by the presentation process. A contractor who held strong views on the need to involve members of his staff in presentations who would, if successful, actually be involved in the scheme believed the process to be about 'the people and not the logo'. Despite the dynamics at play in the interview process, they are essential in a D&B context as they allow the contractor to explain his tender approach in a thorough manner.

Reality check

Examples of best practice in pre-qualification were encountered from a client-led supply chain integration initiative. One of the largest construction clients in the UK has a very proactive approach to selecting suppliers, as part of their 'blame-free' philosophy and use of incentives to drive constant improvement and innovation. The focus on innovation driven by the supply chain and propagated by the client distinguishes it from the majority of D&B encountered in our sample. In this instance, the selection of the supply chain is based on long-term relationships and, as such, the selection process is very well resourced and ultimately does not exclusively depend on capital cost considerations. All the suppliers prepare a proposal and case for their business being included in the supply chain. The distinguishing feature is that the client actively attempts to test the 'reality' of the contractor's organisation that is presented in the pre-qualification document and presentation. This is an attempt to challenge the tenderer's message and is based on the belief that the message communicated by the tenderer's high-level staff has, in experience, sometimes been far from the reality of the situation.

As part of the challenge, the client visits the tendering organisation's offices for the presentation. This gives the client the ability to conduct informal discussions with various levels of staff within the tendering organisation, in an attempt to understand the 'reality' of the situation. As the head of the client team puts it, 'it's about understanding what the organisation is about at the coal face level . . . because everybody can sell in a presentation'. Challenging the contractor in this way takes account of the superficiality of presentations, as discussed previously. The tenderers are scored on many criteria, for example performance, quality, culture, health and safety, and training. The suppliers are given the criteria in advance and this transparent system utilises approximately six to eight questions per criteria. The client team involved in the evaluation process use a scale of zero to five and they are required to justify their scores by giving examples of why they scored as they did. There is a guide question for evaluators, which is asked after the evaluation to try to limit subjectivity. The selection process has other distinguishing features, not least of which is the involvement of other suppliers in the evaluation who have already been awarded contracts. It is carried out in this way as all the existing suppliers will have to work with the successful tenderer and, as such, their knowledge and perceptions are invaluable.

Different approaches to pre-qualification

Pre-qualification processes have been found to vary widely around the world. Palaneeswaran and Kumaraswamy (2001) have studied this

found little evidence of interaction or comparison
:hes. They drew the following examples from across the
are used here to illustrate variations in approach to
1.

Hong Kong Works Bureau

The bureau use an approved list which is split into three categories based
on the contractor's capacity to work on different project values. Further
categorisation confers the contractor with either probationary or confirmed
status. Confirmed status requires previous satisfactory performance on
works bureau projects. The pre-qualification process itself is two stage,
with the first stage being quite broad in nature and intended to screen out
those who are incapable of satisfactory performance. The second stage is a
detailed technical evaluation considering 11 aspects of potential
performance. This example illustrates the importance given to the
approved list of contractors by a large client, itself incorporating an
inbuilt status hierarchy. Unfortunately, the authors do not offer further
details on the structure of the system in relation to the application of
project-specific criteria.

Hong Kong Housing Authority

This authority uses a Performance Assessment Scoring System (PASS) to
review contractor performance on projects. Through the amalgamation of
input/output scores, a league table of contractors allows benchmarking
to take place. A quasi-rotational process is used, which provides
tendering opportunities to those who perform well. Conversely, those in
the lower half of the league table are not invited to tender for a period of
time, with the hope that this will encourage improvement. Embracing the
assumptions of a meritocracy, the system is interesting for its explicit
fusion of benchmarking and opportunities to tender. This approach can
be applauded for the way in which it encourages improvements in
performance through the pre-qualification process.

Queensland Government

This system of pre-qualification criteria (PQC) requires all contractors
wishing to work on projects exceeding (Aus) $100 000 to undergo

generic pre-qualification prior to admission to an approved list. Pre-qualification lasts two years and includes mandatory, additional and reserved criteria. Pre-qualification does not simply end in a binary yes/no decision; but in placement in one of four categories reflecting performance potential.

1. Effective work practices.
2. Commitment to continuous improvement.
3. Industry best practice.
4. World best practice.

It is interesting that terminology used to describe the tender process differs to some extent in Australia from that encountered in the UK. A form of open tendering is used in Australia, although it differs to that previously discussed. Under this method, the contractor must be already registered following pre-qualification and have a risk level that allows him to tender for the project in question. Provided this essential element is met, the contractor can choose to tender for the project, thus increasing competition as the number of tenderers increases. In contrast, select tendering in this context describes the matching of contractors' pre-qualification ratings with an individual project by the client. This results in an invitation to tender for the project with other similarly selected contractors. As with the Hong Kong examples, the centrality of the approved list developed through application of the pre-qualification criteria is highlighted. In addition to simply allowing contractors to tender, it relates the contractor's potential performance ability to different ranges of project risk, such is the range of projects procured by this large-scale client. Under this system, the project value under consideration is also related to the size of the contractor's turnover, a common technique for matching a contractor to a project. Under the quasi-open approach practised in Australia, tendering costs may be high as the client does not limit the amount of tenderers in aiming for maximum competitiveness.

United States — New Jersey and Michigan Department of Transport

The systems in place within these departments are chiefly concerned with determining spare capacity within the contractor's organisation. Having the spare capacity required to be able to complete the works is an important consideration, particularly where the project values can be high placing pressure on the contracting organisation's resources.

This brief journey through various international approaches to pre-qualification demonstrates the importance of the approved standing list in determining who can tender for certain projects. Examples tie the ability to tender to the contractor's actual performance on projects. This may provide UK practitioners with the basis for a similar approach in their own organisations. Benchmarked performance reviews, which are linked to tendering opportunities, highlight the symbiotic relationship between pre-qualification and performance. Pre-qualification exercises assess performance potential through a range of criteria assessing current resource and previous performance. In the same way that assessing project-specific criteria renders the pre-qualification process dynamic, incorporating actual performance reviews increases the overall ability to discriminate and improve information in the decision-making process.

Performance measurement is an increasingly important element of construction management. The Department of the Environment, Transport and the Regions (DETR) has developed various key performance indicators (KPIs). These can be used in pre-qualification and in developing the tender list. Additionally, the Government Construction Clients panel has developed indicators intended to monitor through-life performance of projects. Approaches that tie such initiatives into the ability to tender facilitate performance improvements. Should the client wish to develop his own performance reviews, this requires multiple projects to be procured to amass the historical data. It may also be possible to share data with similar organisations. Alternatively, published KPIs can be used, although standardised performance indicators produced by the larger best-practice bodies have been found to be problematic, as a large-scale client makes clear, 'we tried some published KPIs but we had problems making them work for us'.

The time and effort required to develop approved lists, in addition to that required to continually update the contractor's status, is suited to the repeat procurer of construction products. Not all clients have construction programmes requiring multiple projects and, as such, approved standing lists of contractors are of little use in these instances. Where this is the case, consultants could develop their own database of contractors, taking into account their attributes and performance on previous projects. This is often done implicitly by consultants in an unstructured way, and informs their advice given to clients.

Pre-qualification model

The study by Palaneeswaran and Kumaraswamy (2001) led to the development of a new pre-qualification model which allows project-specific pre-qualification for individual projects, in addition to registration on an approved list. The model embraces the following characteristics.

Binary filter

Application of an initial responsibility, responsiveness and capacity filter, which results in a binary decision to register or reject the contractor.

Dynamic project-specific process

At this stage, the client will develop multiple-criteria based on the individual project and weight these in respect of individual needs. The contractor's attributes are then matched to the criteria in a secondary filter process. The resultant score is numerical and is taken forward to the next stage (see 'Adjustment factor' section below).

Registration on select list

As above, but the criteria are not project specific. They comprise project category benchmarks based on the project values, against which the contractor is evaluated.

As with the binary filter stage, the second stage will reject a contractor not meeting the minimum requirements.

Evaluate workload

This element stems from the importance US practice gives to the contractor's capacity ratings. Providing the contractor's spare-work capacity rating is sufficient in relation to the current project, this will result in a positive binary decision.

Adjustment factor

The output scores from stage two are then used as an adjustment factor when evaluating the contractor's actual tender submission. This type of price/quality mechanism is elaborated upon in Chapter 7.

Although the model as reported was still in developmental stage, it contains important elements in evaluating contractor's performance potential. It allows development of an approved list or project-specific evaluation, and takes account of the weighted criteria and contractor's spare capacity. In isolating the evaluation of broad criteria to an initial stage, which results in a binary decision, and then considering more specific project-related factors in a secondary stage, it shares many similarities with the HOLT approach (1995).

Summary

This chapter has considered pre-qualification in the tendering process. Various mechanisms surrounding pre-qualification were considered and areas of international practice were identified. Several key themes have emerged throughout the preceding sections. First, early client involvement is essential if the pre-qualification criteria are to accurately reflect the nature of the project. Second, although unpopular with some contractors, client advisors need access to accurate and detailed financial information to assess the health of contracting organisations. Third, pre-qualification systems should remain focused and avoid being bureaucratic. Constructing overly bureaucratic systems, or being unable to differentiate between presentation 'spin' rather than competency, are commonly recognised failures within the pre-qualification process. Finally, the ability of pre-qualification to play a crucial role in performance improvement has been outlined.

Chapter 5

Competition in Design and Build projects

Introduction

This chapter examines the nature of competition in Design and Build (D&B) procurement. The classic design competition, where contractors submit different schemes, is considered. However, reflecting on the different types of D&B recognised in Chapter 2, the nature of tendering for developed forms of D&B is also examined. This poses some interesting questions on whether lowest capital cost or best value should be the ultimate criterion for contractor selection. The conceptual and practical difficulties of best-value selection are then explored. This is followed by an overview of some value-management tools, which provide a potential solution to the problem.

Design and Build tendering explained

Tendering for traditional projects generally involves qualification followed by assessment of the contractor's price to build the scheme. This sometimes involves a fusion of these two facets in a price/quality mechanism. However, D&B contains another facet; consideration of the contractor's proposed scheme.

D&B tender evaluation has traditionally been explained in construction texts as a process of evaluating different bids. This view, which relies on the unique factor of disparate contractor solutions in D&B bids is, according to the research data, a little outdated for many projects today. The EPSRC research project on which this book is based, was orientated toward examining procedures to aid client identification of the most suitable D&B scheme from a number of alternatives. This enquiry into the most effective procedures to join client's needs with Contractor's Proposals delivered a surprising finding when viewed in relation to the traditional view of D&B tenders as conveyed in traditional D&B literature. Although examples were found of traditional forms of D&B bidding, which are presented later in the book, they were rare. This dramatically changes the nature of tendering in D&B competitions. Before discussing the emerging issues in D&B tendering, it is pertinent to revisit the classic view of the D&B tender competition.

Accepted understandings of Design and Build tendering

To understand the peculiarities, assumed or otherwise, of D&B tendering, one needs to briefly recall the D&B continuum as explained in Chapter 2. Here, pure D&B is conceptualised as having little pre-contractor design and specification development; in effect, a relatively blank canvas is left for the D&B contractor to develop a scheme that is intended to match the client's needs. The extent of pre-contractor design is generally linked to many different issues, although it is perhaps most strongly related to the amount of control over the project that the client feels they need. Reasons for the reduction in use of pure D&B were discussed in Chapter 2. Literature discussing D&B has generally characterised D&B tendering as a 'design competition'. For example, as recently as 2001, the National Audit Office (NAO, 2001) report into modernising construction still referred to it as 'clients have to specify the type of building they require in terms of the outputs and services it is intended to deliver and the contractor proposes the best design to meet this' (p. 25). Ashworth (1996) holds a similar view of the D&B process: 'With a Design-and-Build arrangement, the client instead of approaching architects for a separate design service, chooses to go directly to the contractor for the all-in design and construction commission' (p. 243). Research in this study found that this type of classic D&B tender competition is rarely used in today's industry.

A typical classic design competition

In this type of classic design competition, the Employer's Requirements are developed highlighting the client's needs. The extent of development differs, for example it may be a simple statement of the size and type of building, or alternatively show elevations, internal layouts, plan views and performance specifications. The Employer's Requirements document defines the client's needs and the contractor responds to these with the Contractor's Proposals document. The Chartered Institute of Building (CIOB) (1988) shows what a typical budget-assessment submission from the contractor, itself possibly forming the first part of a two-stage tender, would have looked like.

1. Design proposal.
2. Outline specification of the building and any external works and services included.
3. A programme of the subsequent stages of the development.
4. An assessment of cost and details of any qualifications.
5. Alternatives offered.
6. Omissions from the brief.
7. List of any prime cost and provisional amounts included.
8. The nature of the price.
9. Supplementary information that assists the client in assessing the likely cost.

Point 7 above needs further consideration. The JCT 1998 Standard Form of Contract with contractor's design requires that provisional sums need to be incorporated in the Employer's Requirements document. Contractors need to raise this point with the client team, as a failure to incorporate means that the contract sum analysis (CSA) cannot be adjusted and the contractor will ultimately suffer financially.

As a respondent to the research study comments, it was often the case in the 1980s that the Employer's Requirements was output based and, as such, was a very slim document with the corresponding contractor's submission being very detailed. This situation has now been reversed in many projects as the same contractor explains:

'the way I've done it in the past if you like is that the Employer's Requirements is a performance brief and the Contractor's Proposals is the detailed specification. This is the way that the original JCT document was written. It wasn't written around the employer coming up with all the drawings and all the specifications, it was written around the employer just saying that he wants a 100 000 square foot office building in such and such a location, and the Contractor's Proposals meeting that.'

Interestingly, this reversal in the use of output requirements is the opposite of current best-practice thinking. Output specifications are more associated with Private Finance Initiative (PFI) schemes and other specialist client-driven procurement routes. Continuing with the classic view of the design competition, the contractor will submit his proposals. Following this, the client is left with the task of evaluating disparate contractors' designs and specification interpretations. The variance in design offered in the Contractor's Proposals differs based on the scope that the client has allowed in the Employer's Requirements and the amount of pre-contractor development that has been carried out. Contractors are given the opportunity to present their schemes to clients, often referred to as a 'beauty parade' following which the client gets the opportunity to ask questions regarding the contractor's scheme. Evaluation of the tenders is generally regarded as being very complex, and has been likened to comparing 'apples and pears', as each scheme will provide a different solution to meet the client's objectives. In addition, the scheme is not fully designed at the time of evaluation, which again complicates the evaluation process. Subsequent to evaluation, the most suitable scheme is selected and the corresponding contractor is appointed, or more suitably given preferred contractor status. This allows the contractor to work with the client to develop the design and specification until such time as both sides are satisfied, a firm price is agreed, and the contractor is appointed.

Selection of the most attractive scheme

As illustrated, the difficult element in the pure D&B design competition is selecting the most suitable scheme from the many options submitted, as all will have different prices and unique properties. The design embodies many different facets, which need isolating and making transparent to aid consideration by the evaluation team. Multi-attribute analysis techniques are generally associated with this type of tender competition. These techniques allow evaluation of different criteria that are developed based on the client's objectives. After the different criteria are developed, including sub-criteria, weightings are applied, relative to the client's priorities for the scheme. These criteria are then used to assess the Contractor's Proposals with scores being recorded by a team of evaluators. This process will typically then combine the score with the price in a decision matrix, using various price/quality equations to determine the proposal offering the best overall 'value' to the client. This type of evaluation matrix is used to aid client decision-making and, as such, can be considered a multiple-criteria decision-making tool. This type of D&B design competition is presented in more detail, together with various options in later chapters.

Another significant component of this classic view of D&B tendering is the utilisation of through-life costing in the evaluation process. The tenderer generally develops the bid based on the scheme's lifecycle costs over a period of possibly 25 years, with the costs being discounted to an easily comparable net present cost. The evaluation of various project attributes, lack of the overriding power of lowest cost, and lifecycle cost component, characterise the classic design-competition selection process as being based on best overall value.

Tendering for developed forms of Design and Build

The difficulty of evaluating disparate bids and the high-tender costs are two of the reasons that the pure D&B tender competition was not commonly found in use in the UK during the research study. Instead, clients are adopting more developed forms of D&B with limited contractor involvement, therefore the pure D&B competition and its associated problems are decreasingly witnessed. One exception is PFI and similar types of procurement that rely on detailed whole-life costing exercises. With developed D&B, the client develops the design and specification to a greater extent prior to contractor involvement, and the contractor is effectively found to be simply pricing the document, resulting in little divergence between bids. The only areas of slight divergence are those grey areas of compliancy and non-compliancy with the client's requirements. These are often a result of contractors finding problems in the Employer's Requirements, or highlighting unfair contract conditions which contractors wish to modify.

The need to allow contractors to input into the scheme

An avenue to allow differentiation between bidders in developed D&B is through offering alternatives, which is discussed in later sections of this chapter. Clients involved in developed D&B projects need to make better use of alternatives because this allows contractors to input directly into projects. Taking into account the reasons outlined in

Chapter 2, clients' inertia to allow contractors much involvement is perhaps understandable. However, alternatives, whether client or contractor led, still allow the client to control projects while facilitating the benefits that giving responsibility and flexibility to the contractor allows. In the later sections of this book, various contractor appointment mechanisms, which are based on the primary data and literature in this area, are offered. An attempt is made to bridge current isolationalist procurement and tendering practices that are generally encountered with pathways to develop contractor input, facilitating overall benefits for the client.

A product of the current move to develop schemes prior to contractor involvement is a separation of the contractor and client relationship. D&B has previously been portrayed as a procurement process with the following relationships:

> Almost without exception in D&B the contractor deals with the client direct. Where the client employs consultants it is preferable that they are used as advisers rather than as agents. This direct contact with the client enables the contractor to have a first hand appreciation of the clients needs, his priorities and his controlling influences.
>
> (CIOB, 1988: p. 6)

The above statement makes clear the early ethos of D&B; that the contractor can access the client's value system and develop a bid on this basis. Unfortunately, developed forms of D&B reduce this possibility, as the tendering process is mainly a pricing exercise. It would seem that much of today's D&B is moving towards the traditional contracting model; that of fragmenting design and construction. Indeed, D&B's ability to fuse design and construction is no longer seen as a driving force by many clients. Instead, D&B is used as a type of traditional contract where the ability to transfer risk is key, as a contractor remarks:

> 'It was all about risk transfer. The design wasn't even important because they had already concluded the design. All they were trying to do was button down the responsibility for both design and construction.'

As pressure aimed at reducing any separation between design and construction continues at a growing pace within the industry at large, it would seem that D&B is in many instances becoming the refuge of isolationalist and backward-looking clients and consultants. Although this is often the case, the EPSRC study has uncovered many examples of best practice. These are generally characterised by contractor involvement, output specifications, well-structured and resourced selection practices, and, above all, trust.

Alternatives

D&B tenders generally allow contractors to forward alternative ways of fulfilling the client's needs. With pure and partially developed D&B, the contractor is allowed flexibility in interpreting the client's needs and, hence, all schemes generally differ and are, by their very nature, 'alternatives'. A contractor will generally offer other alternatives to his 'ideal' proposal, as a type of 'menu pricing' system. Alternatives are important because they allow the contractor to input into the project, thus realigning developed forms of D&B with the original doctrine of contractor integration, value addition and buildability benefits. However, the data suggest that alternatives are often undervalued by consultants and clients and, in certain instances, simply not considered. A project manager with extensive experience representing clients in D&B stresses this point:

> 'The contractor thinks when he puts his price in that he can make money by offering alternatives, and we don't want alternatives, we know what we want.'

Nature of alternatives

Alternatives can take many forms, including such examples as different materials, forms of construction, time frames and programming, or even the desire to use different consultants to those intended to be novated. As mentioned, alternatives become more important as the extent of pre-contractor design and specification development increases. This is because alternatives allow a structured way for the contractor to add input into the scheme and for this to be assessed prior to award of the contract. Although the possibility of alternatives often arise during the actual construction cycle, many arise from sub-contractor input and the focus here is based primarily on those offered as part of the tender submission.

Many alternatives are proposed primarily to offer both clients and contractors the ability to save money, although the data show that the benefits can be far more wide-ranging. For example, programming alternatives can increase client satisfaction in differing ways, such as through earlier provision of a show apartment, leading to earlier sales opportunities. A contractor explains:

'We had a scheme on Friday which was student accommodation, and the end date for us was very very tight, in fact we didn't believe necessarily that we could achieve it. We spoke to the employer and the employer said "well, I'm not so worried about the end date as long as I can have it before the students come back to college, as long as I can have a show flat ready in April". Taking that into account we focused on how we could deliver an April show flat because that enables us to bid an alternative time period that was more comfortable for us to achieve. On that basis we ended up with a different programme altogether, we added another three to four weeks to the programme, but we also added to that programme a show flat earlier in the sequence, so that he could let the units by the time the blocks were ready.'

Where alternative programmes are offered, it requires clients, or consultants working on their behalf, to conduct more than a simple lowest-cost evaluation, even where this forms the end point of any evaluative mechanism. This is true with other types of alternatives, where value needs assessing, and comparing to the 'standard' compliant option. Whether alternatives are embraced for their ability to add value, or viewed as time-consuming activities requiring avoidance, differs between clients and their consultants.

Alternatives — current perceptions

The research study found that one of consultants' overriding objectives is to simplify the tender-evaluation process through ensuring compatibility between tenderers, as an employer's agent makes clear:

'You've got to look at the compliant bid first and make sure that they are all right and base your assessment on that.'

The finding, which is one of the driving forces behind using developed forms of D&B, shows that alternatives are not treated as seriously as they perhaps should be. The following shows a typical tender evaluation on a developed D&B scheme, showing the secondary nature of alternatives.

1. Open bids and identify lowest bidder.

2. Check for degree of compliance, allocation and proportion of costs, and whether the scheme can be built for the sum tendered (is it unrealistically low, leading to potential problems?).
3. Request additional information as required. Should the bid's non-compliance be so great then the bid is disqualified.
4. Following identification of the lowest cost 'best fit' compliant bid, make recommendations and provide the client with a tender report outlining the status of bidders, in addition to attaching any alternative prices.
5. Select on the basis of compliant bid, although any alternatives may be utilised. It is also the case that the client may utilise other contractors' alternatives with the winning tenderer, although this has legal and ethical implications.

What the aforementioned is intended to show is that alternatives are often not treated as an important component of the tender analysis. They are not generally evaluated for their ability to add value but, instead, are attached as a secondary element, allowing the client to save money should they wish to adopt the content of the alternatives. In line with CIRIA (1998), which stresses the need to identify opportunities for contractors to add value, it is believed that alternatives should become a more central part of the selection process. In an attempt to make the tender process efficient, identifying value-oriented activities should not be overlooked. The following factors were uncovered in the data as reasons that alternatives are not taken seriously in many instances.

1. The extra effort in evaluating alternatives. Consultants often complain the time allowed for evaluation of tenders is minimal, so any extra activities would not be possible. This, in turn, is linked to clients often not being prepared to pay for the consultant's time and resources at the crucial pre-contract stage.
2. The client team are often reticent to allow contractors' input into the scheme. Clients, and consultants alike, often believe contractors will only try to maximise their profit at the expense of quality if they are allowed to change the use of materials, etc.
3. Information provided regarding alternatives within tenders is often so minimal that the client team often have difficulty treating them as anything other than a possible cost saving opportunity, which will require more information from the contractor. Requesting more information, and then evaluating it, would use valuable time in an already short pre-contract stage. The reason information is so vague is, first, because contractors are

accustomed to clients sharing their alternative solutions with other contractors in a type of Dutch auction or, alternatively, with the winning contractor to reduce costs. Second, contractors' resources are so stretched in the tender period that anything other than generic outlines are difficult to achieve.

Menu pricing

Alternatives should not be confused with the submission of a bid which does not comply with the Employer's Requirements. The alternatives, which are referred to here, are those offered in *addition* to a compliant bid. Where contractors propose an alternative interwoven with their compliant bid, they potentially run the risk of being disqualified, although, as mentioned, D&B is characterised by grey areas of compliancy. Many contractors interviewed developed alternatives in addition to a compliant bid in an attempt to give them maximum competitive advantage. A director of a contracting organisation involved in the study outlines a typical strategy:

> 'We try and do both. What we do always is try and get the lowest possible quote, lowest price, lowest cost we can. Then we go through a series of proposals whereby we will put forward a compliant at best cost price and then we will also put forward alternatives, which could be said to be better value for money or have different benefits to the client. These can be programme, or a different scheme altogether, whether they be different programme.'

The study found that 32·7% of contractors always offered alternatives as part of their tender submission, while 61·2% sometimes conducted this practice. The perceived importance of producing alternatives is represented in the data, as 80% of contractors believed that offering alternatives helped them to win the tender competition.

Clients will occasionally pre-define their own alternatives in addition to the 'ideal' scheme, in a form of 'menu-pricing'. 24·5% of contractors stated that they were directed into predetermined design alternatives in this way. If one takes the example of a client wishing to seek alternatives for a roof or wall construction, they may allow alternatives to be offered in addition to the standard compliant bid in the following way.

1. A strictly defined alternative, using a prescriptive specification.

2. The contractor is allowed free reign to meet the client's objectives in anyway he chooses. This type of option, utilising an output specification, allows the contractor more input, and most closely mirrors the ethos of D&B.

Such a range of alternatives will usually be arranged to allow evaluation between contractors on simple cost grounds, and the study encountered clients requesting alternatives in both the above forms. It is important that the tendering documents make clear the procedure for submitting alternatives, particularly where the client wishes to implement some type of menu pricing system. Examples of unclear procedures leading to contractors submitting client-defined alternatives as part of their compliant bid were uncovered in the study and often resulted in disqualification.

Contractors' competitive use of alternatives

Many contractors view alternatives as a way of gaining competitive advantage over their competitors, and some adopt a proactive strategy of 'challenging the clients scheme'. On relatively well-developed D&B schemes, contractors often believe that the client's needs could have been met in a more efficient way than that encapsulated in the Employer's Requirements. A senior manager in a medium-sized contracting organisation made the following comment:

> 'You are not party to the development of that concept from inception so you never are quite 100% sure exactly what the client's needs are. You tend to get a bundle of documents that say, "this is the building the client has decided he wants putting up, you just develop the design to the point that you can actually construct it". It's difficult to ascertain, I mean obviously you tend to find once you've hit site, you find out whether or not the architect has actually taken onboard everything the client has requested from him, or that the client has needed from that building, with the number of client change orders that come through.'

Contractors often believe that they are best suited to developing the client's needs into a representative scheme from first principles, although architects often disagree about this:

> 'There is some design development required so you have to go in and dig out the brief. Now builders are not really very skilled at doing that, you know that's not their job, they are builders.'

The empirical evidence illustrates that consultants and contractors often disagreed about who is better suited to develop the client's needs, and many contractors sought to challenge the Employer's Requirements and propose alternatives that, in their view, offered greater value to the client. As mentioned, the amount of time allowed to develop the contractor's tender often does not allow a detailed response. Additionally it is the contractor's belief that it is not in their interest to communicate detailed alternatives. Nevertheless, contractors often conduct value-engineering exercises aimed at developing a better understanding of the client's needs. Ultimately, the benefits of this kind of practice cannot be maximised unless the contractor has direct access to the client's value system. The fact that the consultant team has already encapsulated this in the Employer's Requirements document is not considered a substitute for direct dialogue by contractors. Many contractors attribute winning schemes to a very proactive alternatives policy, and this shows that alternatives are taken seriously by some clients. However, they are often limited to cost-cutting exercises as the extent of scheme development, in tandem with the client and consultant disposition, minimises any greater value addition.

Lowest capital cost or overall value?

What is value?

Calls for increased value have dominated construction industry reports for decades. Terms such as 'value-added', 'value system' and 'value for money' have all become part of an orthodox discourse surrounding the industry. Therefore, before examining methods for increasing value it is worthwhile pausing to consider what is meant by the term 'value'. Value is a complex concept that has occupied academics for centuries. In the discipline of philosophy, central distinctions are drawn in theories of value between subjectivism and objectivism. The former relates value to different states of mind, while the latter accepts that value can exist independently of human beings (Oliver, 2000). Although, at first sight, this distinction may appear to be of little use in practical situations, reflecting on the difficulty of operationalising very subjective personal feelings is very important when establishing formal evaluation systems in the tendering process.

In economics, assumptions regarding the nature and measurement of value are fundamental in many theories. Bannock *et al.* (1998) state that value is the worth of something to its owner. They classify two widely used concepts of value in economics; value in use and value in exchange. Value in use is related to the pleasure a commodity generates for its owner. Value in exchange relates to the quantity of other commodities a commodity can be exchanged for. In contemporary society, this normally refers to money. Therefore, it is obvious that a particular commodity may have a high value in use but a low value in exchange; for example, water. Alternatively, diamonds have a low value in use, for most people they do not perform a useful function, but a high value in exchange. This situation is known as the 'paradox of value' and is widely used in the field of economics to demonstrate that market prices often do not reflect personal notions of value. This is because market prices are determined by both demand and supply, and if a commodity, such as water, is in abundant supply, value in exchange will reflect this.

To contextualise the nature of value in the construction procurement process, it is useful to consider an example. Consider the construction of a new office and workshop development on waste ground on the outskirts of a major city. Value could represent the market price for this development calculated in terms of a discounted rental flow (value in exchange). However, the development may be worth more to the new owner than the market value because the building specifically meets their needs (value in use). This type of value, or satisfaction, is also useful to consider from the perspectives of individual users of the development. Various different users will have different needs and will derive value in different ways. When considering the maximisation of value, various alternative designs satisfy the stakeholders' value systems in different ways. For example, one design solution may increase satisfaction for the owner, for example low-running costs, while an alternative design including more social facilities may increase satisfaction for the other users.

From the above example it is evident that the nature of value and its maximisation is complex. For each building project, fundamental questions need to be asked. These could include the following: is the project attempting to maximise financial market capitalisation, funder satisfaction, principal client satisfaction, user satisfaction, social welfare or professional team satisfaction, or can all of these be maximised in a building project?

Can value be measured?

When a building is completed and in use, is it possible to gauge value, or the satisfaction derived, in meaningful units? If it is not, then how can objective decisions regarding alternative design solutions be made to maximise client satisfaction with limited resources. Bentham (1748–1832), a founding philosopher of utilitarianism, believed that utility or value could be measured on a cardinal scale, and this became a key assumption in early economic theory. A cardinal scale requires satisfaction to be split into units which can be added or subtracted. For example, if wallpaper design A gives the client 20 units of pleasure and design B gives 30 units of pleasure, we can conclude not only that B is preferred to A but that B yields 50% more pleasure than A. These units of satisfaction were later described as utils (Begg *et al.*, 1994). Nevertheless, a major difficulty with representing satisfaction on a cardinal scale lies with the philosophical issues surrounding such measurement.

Most modern economic theory does not rely on the demanding assumption that utility can be measured on a cardinal scale; instead, a less demanding ordinal approach is used. Using the wallpaper example to illustrate ordinal preference, the client could state that design B yields more utility or satisfaction than design A, although we cannot state by how much. Ordinal numbers only rank, and they do not imply distance between ranks, hence the assumption is far less onerous. However, it should be noted that many value-management techniques rely on the assumption of cardinal utility. For example, when various design options are evaluated, a subjective score is often applied against each criteria, these are then added to equate to a final quality score. Although such procedures provide a practical solution and are included later in the text to evaluate non-price factors in design, their theoretical limitations should be remembered when final decisions are made. This is particularly important when quality scores are very close.

The measurement of value is further complicated when economic theories are applied to organisations rather than individuals. It can be difficult to understand organisational needs because institutions are driven by objectives that take into account various external and internal influences. External influences could include government, local population and funders. For example, funding institutions are increasingly involved in the management of the companies they support and will, therefore, affect the direction and mission of the company. When considering value in organisational terms, the complex, and often-competing stakeholder needs, must be appreciated and considered.

One of the most highly promoted modes of best practice in recent years is the call to select members of the project team, whether they be contractors, sub-contractors or consultants, through a process of identifying 'best value' rather than through simple identification of lowest capital cost. 'The primary consideration in the choice of a procurement strategy is the need to obtain overall value for money in the whole life of the service/facility' (HM Treasury, 1999a: p. 3).

Selective tendering and value

As previously mentioned, selective tendering was introduced in the UK to alleviate problems of high-tendering costs and problematic projects, which have repeatedly been linked to lowest-cost competition. In the US, a low-bid philosophy has dominated since the mid-nineteenth century (Harp, 1988, cited by Herbsman and Ellis, 1992) and led to 'extensive delays in the planned schedule, cost overruns, very serious problems in quality, and an increased number of claims and litigation' (Herbsman and Ellis, 1992: p. 142). What the introduction of selective tendering in the UK did was to directly introduce an element of value into the tendering equation. By pre-qualifying contractors, clients could be assured, based on the rigour and focus of the pre-qualification process, that contractors were of a certain quality.

The NJCC code of practice for single-stage selective tendering has, since 1959, promoted final selection of contractors from an approved pre-qualified shortlist on the basis of lowest capital cost. Given the wide adoption of the principles contained in the NJCC codes, industry was being sent the message that lowest-cost selection was the ideal. However, this simple process of an initial quality check followed by lowest capital cost was not seen as effective by many. Industry began to call for selection on the basis of overall value for money, where cost and quality are directly related, and overall operating costs are taken into account. Baker and Osraah's (1985) early study into the factors considered by clients when selecting contractors raises important issues regarding the difference between lowest cost selective tendering and selection on the basis of overall value for money. A resounding 84% of contractors believed lowest price to be the influential factor in determining tender success, while a marginally greater 86·8% of clients based their decision on this factor. This provides an affirmation that the popularity of lowest-cost selection was based on the belief that other factors need not be considered at final award stage, as they have already been taken account of during the pre-qualification process. This explanation corroborates the view that, to some extent, value has always been an essential component of selective tendering in the form of pre-qualification. However, this is not seen as sufficient by factions within the industry who argue that weight should be given to non-price issues at final award stage.

The need to select on the basis of value

The *Code of Practice for the Selection of Main Contractors* (1997), published by the Construction Industry Board (CIB), stresses the need for overall value for money through evaluation of both quality and price. One of the objectives of the Reading Design and Build Forum is to encourage the selection on the basis of value for money. Whether the supposed shift away from lowest cost is being adopted by industry is questionable. Adding to the earlier work of Baker and Osraah (1985), Hatush and Skitmore (1997) found that at bid-evaluation stage it was the lowest bid that decided the winner of the contracts 'irrespective of the technical, financial, managerial and security information available' (p. 32). However, they also found that subjective assessment was increasing in adoption throughout the tender process. In conclusion, they argue that there exists a need to 'clarify and develop predetermined selection criteria, to improve and organise the assessment of information relating to these criteria, and to develop methods for evaluating the criteria against the owners goals in the pre-qualification and bid evaluation stages of the procurement process' (p. 36).

As explained, the pre-qualification process in selective tendering introduces a multi-attribute approach of varying complexities. However, these most recent calls go beyond the initial consideration of contractors' performance potential and instead attempt to balance quality issues with price more directly by introducing some element of cost/quality mechanism to the evaluation of the actual Contractor's Proposals. To be able to conduct such an exercise utilising competition in purer D&B typically involves the following activities. First, the client's value system needs to be made explicit, this can be done in various ways, for example using the principles of value management as explained in this chapter. Essentially, the client's project objectives need making transparent. Second, various ways of meeting these objectives need assessing. Third, following an initial pre-qualification process to assess the contractors' performance potential, the schemes proposed should be assessed in detail. The relationship of the proposal to the client's value system should be assessed by the use of predetermined criteria. Costs should ideally be considered on a whole-life basis and not simply capital cost. Fourth, the tendered cost should be related to the other criteria and this output used to inform the selection of the contractor.

Obviously the client may not wish to utilise a tender competition as described above, instead choosing to negotiate with one contractor directly. Points 1–4 above are based on a holistic approach to differentiating schemes, where the relativity of the various proposals' evaluation scores are maintained and used in the final selection decision. However, an alternative was also found to be used in practice. This approach does not rely on the use of the evaluation scores in the final decision. Instead, following pre-qualification, the client chooses to select on the basis of lowest cost once the proposals (not the organisation as in pre-qualification) have met a target level of suitability. This type of target score evaluation is shown in more detail in the case study of a combined engineering/office facility. Evaluation of this nature illustrates that even with great variation in the bids, clients are able to conduct relatively straightforward evaluation exercises.

Consultants and value

The experience and sophistication of the client need not be a barrier to application of a best-value selection mechanism. Consultants are generally employed to conduct parts of, or all of, the selection process. When consultants are employed by clients in this way, it may seem obvious that they will conduct value-management exercises and employ best-practice selection procedures. However, the data support the view that often construction consultants have minimal practical experience of lifecycle costing, value management, and value-orientated selection mechanisms. An employer's agent who was interviewed confused objectives with solution when discussing the evaluation of bids:

> 'Because we are not being . . . specific, because we are being a bit vague at the moment, it's . . . until you have sat down and gone through the process from beginning to tender returning you only find out during that process what you are looking for, you know what's important.'

This example should be viewed in light of the fact that such procedures are time and resource reliant, and, as such, many clients are unwilling to pay for them. This barrier to demand reduces the need for consultants to be skilled in these areas. In our data, such 'advanced' practices are generally, although not by any means exclusively, the preserve of large-scale well-resourced client departments who utilise both internal and external construction consultants. Nevertheless, the advantages of these kind of practices should ideally fuel greater adoption by clients and, likewise, more proactive marketing by consultants. Thus, current practice is often defined by severance between industry change rhetoric and the often-encountered reality of the situation.

Many contractors complain that the relative importance of the client's requirements are hard to extricate from the Employer's Requirements document, making it difficult to build a representative bid. Numerous examples of best practice advice (CIB, 1997; CIRIA, 1998; JCT, 2002) make clear that where non-price criteria are to be used in the evaluation they should be made clear to tenderers in advance. Where contractors have to undertake elements of design in their proposals, a clear understanding of the client's value system is needed to aid development. Where the client's needs are not made clear, proactive contractors attempt to remedy the situation by building a relationship with the client and virtually interrogating them to deduce their needs. Contractors believe that consultants are neither sufficiently interrogating the client's value system, nor adequately representing the client's needs in the Employer's Requirements document. Making clear the client's marking criteria forces the client and consultants to clarify the client's value system; hopefully an exercise that started early in the value management process.

Pragmatic approach

This book is intended to diffuse areas of best practice in tender evaluation and, as such, it provides practical examples. However, taking into account both the findings of other authors regarding the dominance of lowest cost evaluation and EPSRC data corroborating such practice in the UK, a pragmatic approach is presented in this book. Although evaluating contractors' tenders in relation to the client's project objectives is relatively straightforward, it is also recognised that this advice will not be adopted by many clients and consultants. Consultants involved in the EPSRC study regularly complained that they hardly had enough time to conduct a relatively standard evaluation mechanism. Many clients on developed D&B schemes were simply not interested in evaluating the contractor on multiple criteria once the initial pre-qualification process was conducted; this, for many, would simply mean adding costs to a product that was already extremely expensive.

The less popular pure D&B schemes that result in a design competition require the scheme itself to be assessed and, as such, a multi-attribute evaluation is practically unavoidable, although clients may simply select the lowest-cost scheme which is deemed satisfactory, without initially paying extra to generate long-term savings. Tendering costs are high in pure D&B design competitions and, as such, tendering mechanisms that are overly demanding on resources are not promoted. This is not to say that clients will not benefit from allocating sufficient funds to the tendering process, as to do so will undoubtedly bring benefits. Still, it is recognised that not all clients are so inclined; many regard project funds spent on anything other than the actual physical construction process as more a necessary evil than a way to add value to the scheme. It is accepted that developed D&B awarded by selective competition based on lowest capital cost is widely practised in the UK today. In light of this fact, advice is offered to practitioners and clients to achieve maximum effectiveness from using such a mechanism, such as encouraging contractor input where possible.

Value management in Design and Build tender evaluation

Value management is defined by Kelly and Male (2002) as involving 'the use of a structured, facilitated, multi-disciplinary team approach to make explicit the client's value system using functional analysis to expose the relationship between time, cost and quality' (p. 76). Multi-attribute evaluation of D&B tenders should ideally involve the creation of a client's value system as a measure by which to evaluate the appropriateness of alternative designs. Value management provides a clearly structured process to develop such a value system. The National Audit Office (2001) stated that a limited awareness of value management by clients, and limited use by designers, contractors, sub-contractors and specialist suppliers in the design and planning stage of the project as a major barrier to improving construction performance. However, the majority of publications that discuss value management focus on its use in traditional procurement routes. These publications often refer to the Royal Institute of British Architects' (RIBA) 'Plan of Work' to illustrate the use of value management in the construction process. Taking this limitation into account, the aim of this section is not to provide a comprehensive review of value-management techniques. Instead, it outlines how some value-management strategies and tools can be used to assist those involved in the evaluation of D&B tenders.

Value-management techniques have their origins in the manufacturing sector of the USA. The ideas were focused on the examination of functions aimed at identifying unnecessary cost. Value-management techniques were then adopted by the US military in the 1950s before spreading to the rest of the world. Ashworth and Hogg (2000) point out that various terms used to describe value management are applied inconsistently across various industrial and geographical sectors. They suggest the term 'value management' to describe the entire philosophy and associated range of techniques. Other terms, such as 'value planning', 'value engineering' and 'value analysis', have more specific meanings related to the period of design development when they are implemented. In this book we shall use the more generic term 'value management' because this term is probably most widely recognised by practitioners within the construction industry.

Since the 1990s, value-management techniques have become increasingly accepted within the UK construction industry and through repeated use are becoming more stable and consistent in their application. For example, value-management techniques are typically workshop-based. These workshops are organised by a facilitator who manages the value-management process. The workshops may occur several times throughout the project development or, in other instances, only occur once. Nevertheless, a range of various project stakeholders are normally included to elicit diverse opinions with the aim of capturing the client's value system as comprehensively as possible. Careful consideration needs to be given to the composition of the value-management group, the activities undertaken within the workshop and the frequency of meetings. Research undertaken by Kelly and Male (1998) identified a series of critical success factors, which should be considered when organising value-management activities. These include:

- multi-disciplinary team/appropriate skill mix
- the skill of the facilitator
- a structured approach through the 'value-management process'
- a degree of value-management knowledge on the part of the participants
- presence of decision takers in the workshop
- participant ownership of the value-management process output
- preparation prior to the value-management workshop
- functional analysis
- participant and senior management support for value management
- a plan for implementation.

The quality of the facilitator is a key factor in the success of the value-management process. Short-term cost savings may be realised by opting to confer the facilitator role on a consultant in the project team who is not practised in value management. However, it is our opinion that an external professional who has expertise in value-management techniques will provide a more successful outcome in the long term. This is because he or she will not carry the preconceptions or the possible self-interest inherent in those internal to the project, in addition to being conversant with value-management methodologies.

We have introduced the concept of value management, a concept that underpins one approach to D&B tender evaluation as shown later in the book. This chapter concludes by briefly discussing various contractor selection strategies.

Contractor selection strategies

There are various different ways of evaluating and selecting contractors for construction projects. Many are not made explicit and, as such, can prove ineffective. Holt (1998) provided a review of selection methodologies, which included the following.

Bespoke approaches

Bespoke approaches are particular to a construction client or, as our evidence suggests, unique to individual consultants working on behalf of the client. It is difficult to classify these approaches as they exhibit much variance. Initial investigation to reduce the number of interested contractors prior to pre-qualification involves ascertaining whether contractors meet conforming criteria. This process generally ends in a binary decision yes/no to allow the contractor to proceed to, and be assessed in, specific areas. Holt (1998) notes that the latter stages are generally characterised by subjective judgements, such as the evaluator's previous experience of the contractor. Empirical enquiry shows that consultants place great emphasis on 'gut feeling' during this process, and indeed where they have employed more quantitative measures, this at times has been overridden by a 'gut feeling'.

Multi-attribute analysis

'[Multi-attribute analysis] considers a decision alternative with respect to several of that alternatives attributes' (Holt, 1998: p. 154). The attributes are related to the overall client objectives. This type of selection methodology is widely used to score contractors' attributes, and involves a combination of qualitative and quantitative data. These models can be simply constructed without taking account of the relative importance of client priorities, or include weights to reflect the client's overall project objectives, the latter being advantageous. Holt notes that the biggest problem with this type of model is that they are often based on subjective measures. Although this criticism may be justified, on pragmatic grounds this is still a useful tool. It is this type of multi-attribute analysis model that we propose for use in pre-qualification for all D&B schemes and proposal evaluation in partially developed and pure D&B. Previous authors (Janssens, 1991; CIOB, 1988) have also forwarded similar models for D&B schemes.

Multi-attribute utility theory

Similar to multi-attribute analysis, multi-attribute utility theory incorporates utility into the decision model, and quantifies these values. Utility values are expressed in utils ranging from 0 to 1. These models are often complex to develop because they need to take account of the client's value system on individual projects. They theoretically need developing or altering for each individual project and, hence, practitioners with the requisite skills are required, which can increase evaluation costs.

Other approaches include multiple regression, fuzzy set theory, multivariate discriminant analysis and cluster analysis. However, owing to their lack of adoption by practitioners and generally academic nature, they are not discussed further. The data acquired for this book corroborates the view that bespoke approaches, which are characterised by subjectivity, binary decisions and unstructured process, are most commonly used in industry. Using software-based packages based on the more complex methodologies may result in 'black box' syndrome, where the relevance of the output produced may not be understood by decision makers. Instead, the focus is on multi-attribute analysis, which can be used in its weighted form for pre-qualification and proposal evaluation.

For Holt, the tender process has three stages. First, initial qualification, ending in a binary decision to invite tenders from certain contractors. Second, more project-specific criteria are considered and the contractors are scored on these attributes. Third, the project-specific scores are brought forward to the final evaluation stage, where they are related to price in a price/quality mechanism. The EPSRC study found little evidence of this type of methodology being applied to D&B projects was apparent, although many of the principles are very similar to that used on some relatively undeveloped D&B schemes.

Summary

When comparing Contractor's Proposals in D&B, it is often believed that it is necessary to consider various non-price factors that help determine the overall value of the solution. However, in practice, D&B schemes that are developed to a great extent prior to contractors being involved, virtually mirroring traditional contracting, are often assessed on the basis of lowest capital cost. Understanding the nature of competition in D&B is fundamental to developing a practical evaluation system to determine the optimum proposal. This chapter has explored competition in D&B, but has specifically reflected on how the D&B variant selected impacts on the nature of the competition. Practical considerations, such as the use of alternatives, were also discussed. The nature of value and the assumptions underpinning this concept are central to the selection of D&B proposals. Therefore, the chapter considered these issues before outlining the principles of value-management techniques as a potential tool in the D&B selection process. These techniques are developed in more detail and applied to examples in the final chapter of this book.

Chapter 6

Published guidance, ethical and practical considerations

Introduction

Published guidance should be considered when establishing tendering procedures in a construction project. This chapter begins by outlining JCT *Practice Note Six* (2002) and the NJCC D&B tendering guide (1995), both of which are related to D&B tendering. A recent study heavily criticised some popular codes of tendering practice, including NJCC and CIB guides, and the main arguments are presented to sensitise readers to these potential limitations.

Professionals involved with tendering are often faced with difficult decisions where clear-cut rules may not exist or would be impractical to follow. These decisions are often made by reference to a professional's value-system or ethical framework. Previous studies have shown the range and importance of ethical issues in the tender process, and these ideas are developed in this chapter. Finally, some practical considerations relating to the costs of tendering, both to the individual organisation and wider industry, are considered.

Published guidance

The National Joint Consultative Committee (NJCC) was established in 1954 and has produced many tendering codes of procedure, guidance notes, procedure notes and tendering questionnaires over the years. Although now inactive, study data show that NJCC publications still provide the framework for many D&B tender processes. The now obsolete NJCC *Code of Procedure for Single Stage Selective Tendering* (1959–96), which was developed for traditional contracting, was succeeded by the CIB (1997) *Code of Procedure for the Selection of Main Contractors.* Although not directly relevant to D&B, many of the underlying principles within the NJCC Single Stage Code of Procedure are shared with the more relevant NJCC *Code of Procedure for Selective Tendering for Design and Build* (1995). A relationship made more important as both the CIB and NJCC Single Stage Code have come under recent criticism. It is not our intention to present details of the standard tender documents, as examples of these, including template designs, are provided in numerous other publications.

JCT Practice Note Six. Main Contract Tendering *(2002)*

This practice note is the successor to the NJCC single-stage selective tendering guide (1996a). It also contains elements of the NJCC two-stage (1996b) and NJCC D&B tender guides (1995), which have not been specifically redeveloped in their own right. Although the guide is concerned primarily with 'single stage tendering by a selected list of contractors for contracts where the design responsibility remains wholly or primarily with the Employer and his professional team' (JCT, 2002: p. 2), it also contains provision for design work by the contractor. It states that the preliminary enquiry should indicate whether price will be the sole selection criterion or whether other factors will be considered in the final tender evaluation. It states that 'where criteria other than price are to be used in the assessment of tenders (as opposed merely to being requirements for pre-qualification), those criteria must be set out in detail and the relative weighting of price and the other specified qualities/criteria should be stated' (p. 9). This advice generally reflects the tide of current thinking in this area; that the contractor needs to be made aware of the criteria and their importance to allow them to develop a representative bid. However, the decision to advise that the actual weightings be disclosed to the contractor is not always so readily advocated. Certain clients and their consultants believe that the actual weightings should not be disclosed to the contractors. The logic employed in this decision is based on the belief that contractors will simply develop their proposals and hone their presentations to maximise the marking criteria. A project manager working in a multi-disciplined practice had experienced the following:

'In one instance of this, I actually looked at the tendering, out of 100 points 60 or 70 went to the process and solution side, 30 or 40 went on the price. I actually worked it out that for every one point we answer better on the wordy side we earn a quarter of a million . . . it was a points game, that's all it boils down to, these people like to make subjective things very objective, so they are making things into points. It worked out at a quarter of a million pounds per point. While this may seem the most useful way to approach such an exercise, it is the distrust that clients and consultants have of contractors that leads them to believe that the contractors efforts in this regard will be superficial. To some this means that ultimately it would lead to them simply selecting the contractor who has best manipulated the exercise, the one best skilled in playing the marking game.'

This comment can be related to the earlier discussion of cardinal and ordinal scales for measuring value. This type of problem will, to some extent, always exist in this situation.

Nevertheless, clear identification of the client's value system, including weightings, allows more representative bids to be developed, discussed and evaluated.

Typical non-price criteria include the construction time-frame offered, which can itself provide valuable benefits to clients, in addition to all important functional requirements, aesthetics, lifecycle costs and flexibility in use. Non-price criteria can be assessed at pre-qualification stage or at final-tender evaluation stage. The practice note, aimed as it is at traditional contracting, advocates dealing with this element at the pre-qualification stage where possible, such as to allow the final evaluation to be a relatively straightforward price comparison. Obviously, this is not always possible where elements such as design, functionality and time are included as part of the bid, as in certain D&B projects. The practice note is similar to the CIB (1997) in its advice for schemes where non-price criteria are evaluated on tender submission. It advises evaluating non-price criteria prior to examination of the priced documents, thereby alleviating the importance that can be attached to the price of the bid, prior to understanding the scheme it reflects.

In dealing with qualified tenders, the guide mirrors the advice given in the NJCC guide:

'A tenderer who submits a qualified tender should be given an opportunity to withdraw the qualifications(s) so as to produce a compliant tender, but without amending the price. If the tenderer refuses to withdraw the qualification(s), the tender should be rejected; negotiation of a non-compliant tender is contrary to the principle of equal treatment and in most cases it is impractical at that stage to make other arrangements that would be fair both to the client and to other tenderers.'

(NJCC, 1995: p. 8)

The EPSRC study data suggest that many clients and their consultants would be prepared to negotiate with a contractor who had submitted a non-compliant/qualified tender providing that it was significantly cheaper than the other competitors. 63·9% of clients stated that they would either definitely or occasionally negotiate in this way, while a resounding 81·6% of consultants would definitely do so. This shows that much industrial practice diverges from the advice given in codes of practice.

NJCC Design and Build tendering guide (1995)

The following are considered prerequisites for projects undertaken using D&B procurement:

- the employers should appoint an appropriately experienced and qualified agent and necessary professional consultants
- design responsibilities should be clearly defined without duplication
- a standard form of contract should be used in an unamended form
- the intentions and wishes of the employer should be clearly formulated by the time tenders are invited and set out in the Employer's Requirements upon which the Contractor's Proposals will depend
- great care and attention should be paid to the procedure for the selection of contractors invited to tender
- the information contained in the preliminary enquiry to prospective tenderers should be as full and clear as possible
- the conditions of tendering should be absolutely clear so that all tenders are submitted on the same basis
- adequate time is given to selected tenderers to prepare their proposals
- tenders should be assessed and (if necessary) adjusted strictly in accordance with the terms of the formal invitation to tender.

It could be said that two-stage tender mechanisms lend themselves to D&B, as they encompass development of the project by contractors. However, research data suggest that single-stage selection is the most popular form in use for D&B projects. As previously stated, the NJCC D&B tendering guide suggests that the tender list should contain no more than five contractors at the first stage followed by one or two going through to the second stage. Following a preliminary enquiry sent to contractors, which provides essential project information and elicits their willingness to tender or not, the contractors are invited to an interview. The interview is intended to satisfy various objectives, including:

- determine that the forms of construction, where applicable, to be used by each contractor, will in general be acceptable
- discuss and establish the organisation of work and the time required for tendering
- discuss and establish (if required) the nature and extent of the design indemnity insurance if it is to be taken out by the contractor
- provide any further information required by the firm
- make a final judgement of each firm's competence, bearing in mind the employer's particular requirements and to ensure that those supplying the necessary professional and technical services in connection with the design and detailing will be suitably qualified to prepare the Contractor's Proposals and to complete the design should the contractor's tender be accepted (NJCC, 1995: p. 5).

The interview panel should consist of carefully selected professional advisors who can aid the client in the decision-making process.

Criticisms of commonly applied codes of practice

Craig (2000) has constructively criticised the internal logic of the CIB and the NJCC single-stage documents, and finds them to be inconsistent and incomplete in providing a contractual basis for regulating the tender process. Drawing on recent court rulings, Craig (2000) argues that a tendering code should be developed that has contractual status. This need arises as common law in the UK, Canada and Australia suggests that a tender contract exists after an invitation to tender and a compliant bid. This is because the invitation to tender is now consistently seen by the courts to constitute an offer and not an invitation to treat, as was historically the case, thus a unilateral contract has been formed. However, owing to the privilege clause, the client only needs to consider the bid and not to actually award a contract.

Irregularities and errors

The contradictory nature of the NJCC and CIB codes is drawn out by Craig (2000) in several areas. For example, NJCC advice for dealing with irregularities and errors, following the opening of bids, is that the price cannot be altered without justification, whereas the CIB will not allow the price to be changed on an unaltered scope of works. However, Craig (2000) criticises the NJCC by citing *Vachon Construction Ltd* v. *Cariboo Regional District* [1996] 136 DLR (4th) 307 (Canada), where it was found that an offer on an uncertain price cannot form the basis of a contract without a change in the scope of the works or justification. The internal inconsistency within the CIB document is also highlighted, where, on the one hand, it states that the bidder may request an amended tender price to match the bidder's tender rates, yet simultaneously says that price should not be changed on an unaltered scope of works.

Qualified bids

Considering the issue of qualified bids, Craig (2000) returns to the rule that a qualified bid that does not 'properly respond to the owner's request and stipulations is not responsive (not compliant) and therefore cannot form the basis of a tendering contract' (p. 95). The NJCC seems to conform to this principle by stating that there should be identical tender documents and that bidders should not attempt to vary their bids. However, it simultaneously allows a tenderer, who has qualified his bid, the ability to withdraw the qualifications, which, Craig (2000) contests, effectively allows the tenderer to correct his bid, similar to error and irregularity changes.

Farrow and Main (1996) identify two reasons for qualified bids. First, it is owing to an error or lack of information in the tender document. Second, it is intended to secure competitive advantage. The EPSRC study shows that other reasons are that contractors wish to reject the unreasonable risk-transfer proposed in the Employer's Requirements, and also that the client's budget figure bears no relationship to the scheme encapsulated in the Employer's Requirements document.

The first reason, Craig points out, should be dealt with by informing all tenderers, and allowing tenderers extra time or re-submittal, something that is covered by the NJCC, JCT and CIB codes. However, our data show that, in some instances, contractors believe that if they draw attention to the error, not only is their skill in identifying it lost to other tenderers, but also that, in many instances, the query is neither dealt with nor is an extension of the tender period granted. In addition, as the tender process is competitive, some contractors believe that by keeping the irregularities in the tender documents to themselves they can manipulate the future price of change orders. Hence, certain contractors are sometimes motivated to remain quiet over problems in the tender documents by both of Farrow and Mains's reasons for qualified bids. An example of the lack of information is taken from the data. On many well-developed D&B projects, the Employer's Requirements specify compliance with the Building Services Research and Information Association (BSRIA) regulations for air leakage. However, the acceptable air-leakage figures are often missing from the Employer's Requirements document. When contractors ask for confirmation, they complain that architects often cannot provide the information as they are not conversant with the figures, and sometimes take offence at being challenged for information. Contractors provided this as a reason that bids are qualified, and state that they would prefer not to qualify, but instead be provided with properly drafted Employer's Requirements documents.

Contractors interviewed held the view that if clients did not have the ability to accept qualified bids this would mean that, in the majority of situations, virtually every tender would be rejected as qualifications are so common. D&B requires interaction between the client team and the contractor, something that the NJCC alternative one and two does not take account of. It should be noted that the JCT *Practice Note Six* (2002) states that alternative one is not appropriate for two-stage tendering. Nevertheless, bids which are qualified in any way effectively alter the baseline of comparability between bids, and again this is an area where D&B tender evaluation is complex. Farrow's earlier work is similar to that of Craig (2000):

> The professions who are normally under instruction to invite tenders usually do not like to receive tenders which have been conditioned, i.e. having one or more conditions attached to them either amplifying, clarifying or denying some statement in the instructions to tender. This is understandable and conditions can lead to inequalities of comparison and other difficulties. Any obvious matters leading to conditioning should have been dealt with in the preliminary invitation stage or on receipt of tender documents.
>
> (Farrow, 1993: pp. 4–5)

Contractors interviewed cited that a common reason for qualified bids is the unreasonable terms and conditions that are encapsulated in the contract documents by the client's consultants. According to contractors, clients often do not realise the nature of the terms and conditions that the contractors are being asked to comply with. Many clients, when confronted with the onerous nature of the contract documents understand why contractors wish to qualify them.

The research underpinning this book found an example where consultants requested a £10 000 bond from contractors to ensure that they did not forward any type of qualifications. However, the contractors who were tendering for this particular project found this to be extremely unfair and effectively unworkable. This is because although in D&B the scheme is often developed to a similar extent to traditional contracting, it is common for there to be an oversight in the Employer's Requirements, such as design or specifications that do not comply with building regulations. On this particular scheme, there were many such mistakes. This example, utilising a £10 000 bond, underlines consultants' extreme aversion to qualifications. As stated, contractors complain that dealing with such anomalies during the tender period is difficult as tender periods are usually too short. In our data 58% of the contractors informed the client of anomalies at tender stage. 38% of contractors simply stated qualifications in their Contractor's Proposals when they found discrepancies in the tender documents.

The issue of what to do with a qualified tender is unclear from the literature. For example, Farrow (1993) seems to believe that it is the degree of non-compliance that is key: 'If these additions are so onerous (i.e. risks that cannot be properly evaluated and quantified), they should only be dealt with by rejecting the invitation . . . A tender that does not comply (i.e. conditioned) with the invitation to tender is nevertheless a valid offer. The refusal of a conditioned offer is a risk the contractor has to take' (p. 5). This view was shared by a director in a regional contracting organisation interviewed as part of the EPSRC study, who held the view that 'a bid is a valid offer able to be accepted, refused, or negotiated upon'.

However, this pragmatic view stating that a non-compliant qualified bid is a valid tender that is able to be accepted seems to contradict Craig (2000) who, drawing on case law, specifically *Pratt Contractors Ltd* v. *Palmerston North City Council* [1995] 1 NZLR 469 (New Zealand), states that: 'It is submitted that, without appropriate stipulation in the tender conditions, there are no circumstances where the owner can do anything other than reject qualified (non-compliant) tenders. To consider, or even accept, a qualified tender would amount to a breach of the equal and fair treatment obligation' (Craig, 2000: p. 96). Craig (2000) finds the NJCC deficient in its advice on this issue to allow tenderers to withdraw and qualify bids. The NJCC agree with the CIB advice to reject non-compliant tenders, which are not received in conjunction with compliant bids, as it removes 'any discretion for the owner on this point' (Craig, 2000: p. 96). However, in D&B tendering, especially purer D&B, the nature and degree of compliance is something of a grey area. Many contractors interviewed believed that in the majority of instances bids are rarely 100% compliant, as to do so would minimise the potential to negotiate more reasonable terms and conditions as the basis of the contract. As Turner (1995) points out, the Contractor's Proposals are often very complex and, as such, can often constitute a counter offer.

Ethics in tendering

Crisp (2000) outlines three related and hierarchical meanings of the term 'ethics'. First, to refer to a broad system of values characteristic of certain human communities. Second, to refer more specifically to one value system; that of morality. This involves evaluating what constitutes 'right' and 'wrong' decisions. Third, within a system of morality, ethics can be used to refer to the actual moral principles. So, what impact do ethics have for professionals in the construction industry? Ethics are central to the concept of professionalism and serve to distinguish those occupations that claim professional status from those that do not. Professionals within the construction industry, for example architects and surveyors, are required to adhere to codes of conduct set by professional bodies. However, the manner in which professionals practise on a daily basis is more likely to be guided by a basic ethical framework rather than reference to a rule book. Therefore, it is essential that an ethical framework is shared within a professional community and that these principles effectively guide individual decision-making in the practical management of construction projects.

Major studies

In this instance, consideration is given to ethical issues in a business context. Authors over the years have forwarded the notion that ethics and effective business practice are irreconcilable concepts (Friedman, 1982). Ray *et al.* (1999) have studied the ethics of tendering by surveying the Australian construction industry. 77% of those surveyed in the Australian study used a standard code of ethical practice, whether externally published or developed in-house. Ray *et al.* isolate five major ethical issues in tendering, as follows.

Withdrawal

Tenderers have the right to withdraw a bid prior to formal acceptance. However, on occasions this ability is abused and otherwise satisfactory bids are withdrawn when another, more seductive, business opportunity is available to contractors. This may, in severe circumstances, lead to re-tender costs, and wasted evaluation processes. However, owing to the typical situation of short tender periods, and submission of bids close to the cut-off period, this practice is very rare. Their data showed that a majority of respondents (88%) believed that the ability to withdraw was fair and should continue.

Bid cutting

Bid cutting is used to describe the process of trying to reduce sub-contract prices prior to and following award of the contract. The majority of respondents (72%) believed this practice to be unethical after the award of contract, where contractors revisit their sub-contractors in an attempt to reduce their costs. These cost savings are often not passed on to the client, and are intended to increase contractor profit. However, where the contractor is motivated to follow such practice because he believes the sub-contract package price is disproportionately high, or high-risk, responsibility forces such practice, Ray *et al.* (1999) believe the practice is understandable. It is the intention of the contractor that is important here. The National Audit Office (2001) identified sub-contractors' prices being forced down by a Dutch auction as a major barrier to improving construction performance. Our data suggest that sub-contractors are so accustomed to the practice of bid cutting following the award of a contract that they artificially inflate the price given to the contractor at tender stage. While taking into account the lack of perfect information used in the estimating process when developing the sub-contractor price, this theoretically results in an artificially inflated tender price for the client. However, main contractors take this inflation into account during final tender decisions, thus modifying any potential inflation. Bid cutting is also associated with confidentiality problems, where a contractor may openly divulge a sub-contractor's price to others in the hope that they will undercut it.

Cover pricing

Universally criticised, this practice involves submitting a price that is not intended to win work, but is intended to appear competitive. Five somewhat interrelated reasons are given for this practice.

1. Little interest in the contract.
2. Lack of resources for the project.
3. Not enough time to develop adequate tender.
4. Desire to remain considered for future sales.
5. Large number of firms reduces the probability of winning.

However, a contractor interviewed as part of the EPSRC study added other reasons.

6. Nature of competition — which refers to contractors gaining knowledge, through sub-contractors, that certain other contractors are determined to win the project by bidding a very low price for various commercial reasons.
7. Revised tender issue — this describes the scenario where the tender documents are issued late and, hence, contractors' estimating staff have moved on to work on other projects.
8. Scope of tender different to that anticipated — for example a new build scheme could have been changed for a majority refurbishment scheme at a late stage.
9. Terms and conditions — these may prove too onerous once the alterations to the standard form of contract have been taken into account.
10. Changes in the client's funding — may make contractors less interested in winning the contract.

It is generally considered that the fourth reason is the overriding aim of this practice. Cover pricing reduces competition, as it effectively reduces the number of genuinely competitive bids, in addition to the possibility of encouraging collusion. It can also prove extremely problematic where, for whatever reasons, the contractor who submitted the cover price is selected for the contract.

Compensation of tendering costs

Particularly pertinent to D&B tendering: who should absorb these costs? Various publications suggest recompensing the contractor where tendering costs have been particularly high. It is an accepted part of some US projects that the client pays the contractor for his proposal and, in doing so, the client retains ownership of the design. One only need consider the massive tendering costs that can be accumulated in a conventional D&B design competition to understand the need to provide some form of compensation to contractors for considerable expenditure.

Whether this is a business or ethical issue is debatable, but whatever its basis, tender costs not met will need to be recouped on the contractor's next successful project.

Collusion

In this context, collusion is predominantly used to refer to an arrangement reached between tendering contractors with the intention of affecting the tender competition. For example, a group of organisations will collude to determine a tender price to be submitted by one of them that is the lowest price and, hence, likely to be accepted by the client. Three issues are highlighted in this practice.

1.   It provides an even distribution of work for colluding organisations.
2.   The tenders appear to be *bona fide* to the client.
3.   It provides a way of agreeing illicit profits.

In the 1999 Australian study (Ray *et al.*, 1999), just over a quarter (27%) of those surveyed were directly aware of collusive practices. The EPSRC did not uncover actual collusive practices, although some consultants do work for more than one contractor during tender development, which can in itself be problematic. In this instance, tendering contractors who are required to develop designs for the purposes of a D&B tender competition will routinely employ the services of external design practices. One practice may well work for numerous contractors in the tender development stages of one project. Thus, the design firm can, albeit unintentionally, disseminate cost-based information between contractors. For this reason, and other confidentiality issues revolving around design, the practice of providing design services for more than one tendering contractor is not promoted here.

Disseminating the Contractor's Proposals

In addition to the aforementioned issues, D&B has additional ethical implications centred mainly on the contents of the Contractor's Proposals. In purer forms of D&B, the client obtains, effectively free of direct charge, a number of different scheme developments. If more developed forms of D&B are utilised, the client often still obtains varying bids from contractors in the form of alternatives; again, free of charge. The client is then in a position to trade information between contractors to reduce prices, or to assemble the most advantageous scheme.

When considering the confidentiality of information, the CIOB code of estimating practice for D&B projects (1988) states that:

All documents submitted as part of a tender should be treated by the client and his professional advisers as confidential and not disclosed to any third party without the contractors consent.

(CIOB, 1988: p. 35)

The JCT *Practice Note Six* provides similar advice. It states that:

Any designs and design information supplied by unsuccessful tenderers should be returned to them . . . Information supplied by unsuccessful tenderers that is not in the public domain should not be used for any purpose by the employer or its advisors.

(JCT, 2002: p. 9)

This may seem obvious advice, however, practising such a dictum is more complicated than it first appears when the peculiarities of the D&B tender scenario are taken into account. Where there are multiple disparate proposals, the very act of asking contractors clarification questions during scheme development could disseminate design proposals between all tendering contractors. Obviously this scenario is not ideal as it gives unfair advantage to the other contractors, in addition to narrowing the variance in schemes, itself often seen as the basis of such a design competition. Janssens (1991) offers a potential way round this problem, he recommends using a questionnaire to structure clarification enquiries.

Should the client choose to negotiate with one contractor, this allows an open dialogue between both parties, with elements of interaction from the client's consultants. However, when the client chooses to utilise competition, particularly in pure D&B, the situation becomes more complex. This is because of the need for equity and parity between bidders. Although the client's needs are encapsulated in the Employer's Requirements document, contractors generally liaise with the client and his consultants to gain a better understanding of the client's needs. The contractor's proposed scheme is built up in an iterative manner, using his design team. The design team can be both internal or external, and include sub-contractors and suppliers. The EPSRC investigation discovered that the number of contractors who retain a permanent full-time internal design team is quite low; only 31·4% having such staff. A contractor explains his organisation's decision to disband its internal design team:

'We took the view very much that we would get more work by using external consultants. Like most major contractors, there's very few major contractors now who have their own design offices. Clients certainly nowadays don't trust design and build contractors that have their own designers. They want that professional consultant input from not necessarily a totally independent consultant, but somebody who is going to put his professional indemnity on the line and design something of quality. The opinion of the design and build contractor is he's always going to be looking on the cheap side.'

However, it should be noted that not all clients distrust contractors who retain internal design staff and, in many instances, the reason to disband is purely a business decision based on reduction of overheads. Interaction with the client and his consultants is an essential part of the process, and many contractors believe it necessary, even with developed D&B, to challenge the scheme developed by the client's consultants, as previously stated. However, the possibility for dissemination of contractors' ideas between different bidders is great. Turner (1995) notes the usefulness of dialogue between the client and tendering contractors, yet believes it needs controlling to maintain parity.

The client needs to safeguard against transfusion of contractor designs, both from an ethical standpoint, and to increase the competitive element. Transfusion will lead to a homogenising of the design and, hence, the potential for design differentiation is minimised.

It is often the case that during tender development in purer forms of D&B that the contractor liaises with the client to gain his impressions of the developing design, or to more directly assess his value system and project objectives. Indeed, this is encouraged — the closer one gets to the client's needs, the more effective the product of the relationship. However, as stated, dialogue needs controlling. For example, it could be the case that one contractor has recently visited the client with a particularly innovative way of meeting a particular design issue. Should another contractor then approach the client to similarly discuss scheme development, it is easy for the client to divulge the nature of the previous contractor's interpretation of his needs, whether intentionally or not. If done intentionally, the client's motivation could be the belief that it will get the most from the process. Drawing on the Copyright, Designs and Patents Act 1988 and the definition of artistic work, which includes drawings, plans, models and buildings, Turner shows how such work is protected by copyright law. However, despite the existence of this seemingly secure retreat for contractors, the Act refers to actual work and not ideas without material form. Turner shows the issue to be problematic:

He (the client) can hardly insulate one design from the other in his mind, so that he is bound to carry ideas over from one to the other. However, it is no defence against infringement of copyright to plead that a part of one design was abstracted as an *idea*, which was then injected into another design, so that *copying* did not occur.

(Turner, 1995: p. 84)

Despite the somewhat nebulous legal position, it is unlikely, on a typical project, that a legal course of events will be resorted to. Owing to the iterative nature of design development, it is difficult to delineate individual design ownership until final designs are submitted. However, once this stage is reached, the problem of confidentiality is by no means avoided. The client, in purer forms of D&B design competition, typically receives numerous different bids regardless of any cross-contamination at the tender development stage.

Irrespective of the stage at which design sharing takes place, respondents in the data highlighted how easy it is for a client at this stage to take elements from different bids and mould them into the foundations of the contract with the selected contractor. This, it was stated, is easy as contractors do not have access to 'behind the scenes' final selection negotiations. Once the contractors are of no further interest to the client they are, in a number of instances, simply informed by post, if at all, without any form of debrief. It is only months later when unsuccessful contractors pass a completed project and see what they believe to be their ideas taking a physical form that alarm bells begin to ring.

Of those clients surveyed during the research, 80·6% would either definitely or occasionally share contractors' ideas with the winning contractor. Although consultants indicated they were less likely to conduct such activities, a still overwhelming 66·7% indicated that they would act similarly. This problem is not limited to purer forms of D&B.

In developed forms of D&B, where contractors submit alternatives, the client can, if so inclined, just as easily highlight such options to the selected contractor despite the legal and moral/ethical implications. Such practice is deplored and it has been found repeatedly in the research data that the client, in using such underhand practices, is ultimately cheating himself. This is because contractors become less and less inclined to be open and transparent in their dealings with clients. Trust is diminished, and with it all the benefits that a collaborative approach can bring.

Fortunately, not all clients utilise such practice, but discussion of these possibilities is intended to sensitise the reader to the issues. Central lessons of best practice include:

- design sharing at final appointment stage, unless it is implicitly tied into the tendering mechanism with the client owning the design at this stage in return for a design fee, is not advised
- clients should attempt to limit the potential of sharing contractors' ideas at tender development stage — recording the nature and outcome of interaction can aid this aim.

Contractors who were involved in the EPSRC study outlined various ways to prevent their ideas being disseminated on to the marketplace, although the practicalities of applying them are often not straightforward.

1. Only make alternative ideas available to the client when they are considered the successful contractor. Note that this is not following contract award, but during final negotiations, and it is considered a way of making the bid more attractive.
2. Limit the information made available. Limiting the information may indeed result in the bid not being taken seriously by the client, or indeed the client may request additional information to clarify the offer.
3. Do not present any design solutions until reasonable assurances that the information will not be disseminated on to the marketplace have been given. Obviously this represents a risk for the contractor, and the client's ethical stance is important.
4. Monitor schemes whenever the contractor is not selected to gauge whether their ideas were used on the scheme. This creates a benchmark for future relationships with the client.
5. Pay the contractor's tender development costs, effectively paying for the contractor's design expertise and being able to use it as required.

Design and Build — an inherent propensity to cut corners to increase contractor profit?

Additional ethical issues have been raised in the US. These issues follow a different orientation to those already discussed, and principally revolve around the degree of flexibility that the contractor is given to mould scheme development. Zechman (2000) discusses the ability for the contractor to profit through quality reductions in D&B:

> The contractor has the opportunity to cut corners on the design to bid at a lower price, using smaller structures that just meet the design requirements and low quality materials. If the contractor takes advantage of the situation, the owner will lose control of the quality of the design. It becomes the responsibility of the contractor to provide his own checks, his own ethics, to avoid taking advantage of the owner in design-build construction.
>
> (Zechman, 2000: p. 102)

This statement needs conditioning by an understanding that the extent to which the contractor can take these design and material decisions is controlled by different factors. For example, the Employer's Requirements document and the extent of development left to the contractor, in addition to the general checking process leading to the scheme as defined at contract award. However, in providing the opposing argument, Zechman herself draws on the overriding concern of those in the US construction industry; to behave in a deceptive manner and cut costs leading to a low-quality product will result in 'corporate suicide' for the contractor. The data from the US element of this study supports the view that contractors take seriously the link between client satisfaction and their image and future work possibilities.

Whether the way in which the contractor meets the client's requirements is an ethical issue or simply a contractual one is debatable. The identification of a contractor who will actively seek to provide client satisfaction will reduce any potential 'corner cutting'. Whereas Zechman mediates the negative view of D&B as a cost-cutting procurement route with the view that contractors need to satisfy clients to achieve future work, Bruce (2000) holds the view that D&B overtly leads to cost predominating over quality, in comparison to traditional contracting where he believes best value can be obtained. This rather naive and biased view is a result of considering the ethical code of procedure that engineers follow in traditional contracting in the US.

> The traditional system incorporates an internal checks and balances system by allowing the owner to choose the contractors based on the 'best value bid', a bid that has been determined from a set of plans and specifications previously prepared by the design engineer and approved by the owner.
>
> (Bruce, 2000: p. 103)

Based on US practice, the logic of this statement needs challenging. Simply because the client has opted to utilise a traditional form of contracting does not mean that they will choose an overall scheme that offers best value for money any more than the use of a D&B scheme results in the opposite. It is the client's objectives, design team interpretations and outputs that shape the scheme as tendered. The internal checks and balances are theoretically no more a consequence of procurement type choice than is identification of the most suitable contractor. Nevertheless, Bruce (2000) continues, 'The unique relationship between the design engineer and the contractor in design-build projects inherently promotes cost cutting. In many cases cost cutting produces a reduced quality and/or a sacrifice of public safety' (p. 103).

Simplistically linking contractors' involvement in design development in D&B to an almost automatic breach of ethical principles in this way provides an interesting reference point for many of these perceptions in the UK. For example, the view that architects and engineers adhere to more ethical practices, and behave in a more professional way, was evident in the EPSRC studies data. An architect's view shows a typical perception:

> 'It always will, quality will reduce when an architect is working for a building contractor, at the end of the day they are out to make money.'

Contractors were often perceived by architects as not subscribing to a satisfactory ethical framework. However, the fact that the majority of contractors sampled held similar qualifications and were members of a professional body with its own ethical code of conduct seems to be overlooked. While discussing the popularity of D&B, a senior manager in a contracting organisation made the following observation:

> 'I think it is just the whole ethos of building a professional team. Actually recognising the construction side of the team as professionals as well as historically the architect, the engineer and the other consultants, actually recognising the builders as professionals.'

Having considered various ethical issues that occur in D&B tendering scenarios, we turn our attention to explore some practical considerations relating to the costs of tendering and whether to utilise competition.

Practical considerations

Tender costs

Tender costs in D&B have always been regarded as being higher than those amassed in tendering for traditional contracts. This is linked to the classic view of the design competition requiring contractors to use resources to develop submissions, which then need time and resources to evaluate.

An example of high-tendering costs was offered by a US practitioner interviewed as part of the study. He referred to a US Federal General Service Administration (GSA) scheme he had been involved in. The $200 million data processing centre in Detroit utilised 11 D&B teams who spent 18 months each tendering for the scheme. This wasteful use of resources was estimated to have cost each team $500 000, and was rationalised as it was the first type of scheme that the GSA had procured in such a way. The contractors' tender development costs are partly a function of the extent of the scheme development required. In the US, the norm for scheme development is roughly 30% (Denning, 1992). There is no average figure available for UK D&B, possibly understandable as it is difficult to both generalise and isolate the stage where the design development ends for tender purposes. One way of reducing tender costs is to reduce the tender list in stages as the tender process develops.

The NJCC *Code of Practice for Selective Tendering for Design and Build* (1995) advises a final tender list of not more than three firms and, where two-stage tendering is used, this should begin with five to six contractors and reduce to one to two in the second stage. Typically in two-stage tendering, the second stage will involve one preferred bidder developing the scheme, thereby reducing tendering costs. One contractor is typically kept in reserve should talks breakdown. Where a single-stage D&B design competition takes place, possibly with three to four tenders being involved, costs can be very high. Some clients recompense contractors for part or all of their tendering costs, although this practice was not found in the EPSRC data.

As the client-side evaluation team usually needs at least four members to demonstrate representativeness and allow stakeholder input, the cumulative time required can be considerable. The research data contain an example of a railway rolling stock facility, which was competitively tendered. Despite its technical nature and highly developed output requirements, the contractors were given great flexibility in their proposal development. One interviewee, a high-ranking manager within one of the contracting organisations tendering on their scheme, estimated his organisation's input costs, including those of outsourced work, to be £100 000. Considering that the other four bidders would have all spent approximately the same amount, in addition to the cost of evaluation which took account of lifecycle costing issues, the cumulative waste of tendering resources is significant; costs which lead to tender inflation and overall industry inefficiency.

Owing to the fact that many contractors do not have their own in-house design teams, this proposal development work is outsourced to sub-contractors and design teams, who often work on a speculative basis. Outsourcing work 'at risk' in such a way is generally considered to be problematic:

> 'We don't like it and we certainly have reservations unless we know the client, even so perhaps we are a bit soft, it worries us at times. Converse is we've got a lot of work on and so yes our bankers keep on castigating us saying we take too many risks in that way, we take schemes too far. However, for a great many developers the skill is knowing how not to pay anyone.'

To compete or not to compete?

Turner (1995) argues that here is a prima facie argument for competition as far as the client is concerned, while simultaneously recognising a similar argument against competition for contractors. For clients, competition offers the free-market principle of reducing costs, while for contractors it reduces the probability of winning the contract in addition to risking the costs involved in developing and pricing a design. It should be noted that increased use of developed forms of D&B reduces the contractor's tender development costs.

The UK construction industry appears to be diverging over whether competitive tendering is used or not. It would seem that while many smaller-scale contractors still rely on competitive tendering, many large-scale contractors have decided to discontinue their involvement in competitive tendering. A senior D&B manager within a large nationwide contracting organisation describes how his organisation secures work:

> 'There is a significant change in the way that the industry is actually operating, and a lot of the major contractors have gone out of competitive tendering altogether. It's certainly not something we will do because we are not a major contractor, we are in the top 20, 25, but certainly not top 10, and so I would say that half of our work is competitively won. However, the other half is through negotiation, partnering, framework agreements, and PFI type routes.'

The contracting organisation's propensity to become involved in competitive tendering is partly affected by the strength of the economy. The study data suggests that a thriving economy often means that organisations can be more selective in which contracts they choose to tender for, with non-competitively secured contracts becoming more popular. A contractor makes clear his thoughts on this issue:

> 'Clients at least now acknowledge that there is a lot of waste in the tendering process and contractors don't have to bid everything and anything as they can be selective. That is one of the reasons clients are looking at partnering and framework and supply chain management processes because they are not necessarily getting the best value for money by going through a competitive process.'

A booming economy often results in what some contractors consider to be small and inexperienced contractors being included on the tender lists for projects they would not normally be tendering for, and this can lead the more regular, experienced tenderers to decline to bid. One contractor explains his position:

> 'Our organisation and others are able to select which lists we want to be on, or which projects we want to do. When the economy is strong we get the smaller companies who are perhaps not up to a design and build situation, and are not professional. That's when we get these people creeping into the list. You know if you are in a competitive market against those companies, you know you are wasting your time really and that is not being derogatory to those companies. You need to realise that there's different levels for different companies you know and you don't want to be pre-qualifying for a £15 million job if you've got a reasonable [emphasis on reasonable] construction company whose biggest job is only £2 million and that has happened. You know that you are wasting your time.'

Summary

This chapter has considered issues surrounding published guidance in relation to D&B tendering. Two major publications were discussed — JCT *Practice Note Six* (2002) and the NJCC D&B tendering guide (1995). Criticisms of these codes of practice were discussed highlighting the difficulties surrounding compliant and non-compliant bids. The second substantive area covered in this chapter related to ethical considerations in the tendering process. Five major areas were identified. These included withdrawal, bid cutting, cover pricing, compensation of tendering costs and collusion. Finally, the problems associated with the dissemination of contractors' design solutions by the client to a contractor's competitors were considered. The chapter concluded by outlining some practical considerations with specific reference to the costs involved in tendering.

Chapter 7

The practical application of best practice tendering

Introduction

The final chapter of this book draws on earlier themes and applies them to the practice of Design and Build (D&B) tender evaluation. This is developed through several major sections. First, building on the concepts introduced in Chapter 5, different types of D&B tender competition used in practice are considered in detail. Second, various contractor selection models are presented which can be used as a basis for evaluating D&B tenders. Separate details of value management and lifecycle costing techniques are then discussed. The focus is on the application of these tools and various examples are given to illustrate how practitioners can integrate these techniques within the tender process. The chapter finishes with the presentation of a case study showing a typical D&B project that was encountered during the research study.

Types of Design and Build tender competition

As discussed previously, multi-attribute evaluation is applied during pre-qualification, both general and project specific, and possibly at proposal evaluation. The research data show that multi-attribute evaluation tends only to be employed during proposal evaluation where pure and some partially developed D&B is used and, hence, there exists substantial differentiation between Contractor's Proposals. It is this aspect of evaluation which is the focus of this section, although the result of the pre-qualification exercise itself can be brought forward and used in the final tender-assessment to balance price and quality as in Holt's approach (1995).

Flexibility of the Employer's Requirements

The Contractor's Proposals will vary based on the amount of flexibility the Employer's Requirements allow. In addition, compliance is determined by the degree that the contractor can comply with problematic Employer's Requirements, and how advantageous contractors decide it is to deviate from the document. While an output-based specification is preferable, many clients wish to tightly define certain elements for numerous reasons. Irrespective of the extent and prescriptiveness of the Employer's Requirements, the brief should make the client's needs as explicit as possible, with value management being promoted in this end and expanded on later in this chapter. This should not be confused with making the Employer's Requirements overly prescriptive; the scheme can be output based and still encapsulate the client's needs very clearly and precisely. The client may wish to forego competition and directly liase with a contractor and negotiate a price. Some clients interviewed in the study still opted for the contractor who declared the lowest overhead and profit figures during discussions, however, these figures can often be manipulated and evidence of their build up is critical to understand the 'fuller story'. Negotiation offers the potential for better overall value, including benefits such as a better understanding of the schemes and, hence, lower risk, better relationships and improved planning of schemes, which can, in turn, lead to shorter construction times and outturn costs.

Various forms of Design and Build

Should the client wish to competitively tender a pure D&B scheme, there are numerous options, all of which should contain a detailed pre-qualification element. When referring to a two-stage tender, it is noted that different stages are often unclearly defined, if defined at all. Some contractors complained that it is often clear that the client team has not developed a structured-tendering process and tends to 'make it up as they go along'. Turner (1995) similarly acknowledges this lack of accuracy, 'Mention has been made of two-stage competition and logically there may be quite a number of stages, however imprecisely they may be identified' (p. 106). A number of possible different approaches are laid out below and all assume a pre-qualification process has already taken place.

Two-stage tender — pure Design and Build and partially developed initial proposals and preferred bidder

The first stage can take many forms, for example documents pricing the client's initial scheme development or an indicative outline scheme developed by the contractor including some form of cost benchmarks. The contractor could provide indicative prices for different elements, which can form the basis of negotiation in the second stage.

Initial proposal development
In cases where the contractor develops an indicative scheme, it will typically have been shaped by an iterative design development process during which the contractor interacts with the client and his consultants. Contractors are reticent to divulge too many details at the first stage as they fear losing competitive advantage, with many complaining that the client can easily abuse the process. It also needs considering that many contractors do not develop any designs at tender stage and, instead, simply submit a very simple tender return outlining a price for the scheme. These type of bids do not allow a like-for-like comparison between contractors, and are often submitted with a low capital cost to tempt clients.

Whatever the nature of the tender submission, an indicative price is proposed and the contractor typically presents his scheme to the client providing a sales opportunity. The schemes are generally evaluated using multi-attribute evaluation mechanisms where all the different schemes are compared for their ability to meet the client's project objectives. The preferred bidder then goes through to the second stage and develops his scheme in close collaboration with the client.

Initial pricing without scheme development
In this scenario the contractor will typically price the client's initial design. As with the above type of two-stage tendering, a secondary bidder is kept involved in the project should negotiations breakdown with the preferred bidder. Compensation of both the preferred and secondary bidders costs, and clarification of copyright issues, should ideally be incorporated into agreements to ensure the best service is maintained. After the scheme is sufficiently developed, and the client

and contractor have agreed a price, the contract is awarded and construction can begin. This arrangement seeks to minimise the contractor's tendering costs as it limits the amount of work done in competition to the first stage. The second stage allows the scheme to be developed to a relatively great extent and, indeed, this is important as it allows both parties to determine clearly the terms of the agreement and understand in greater detail the product that is being purchased.

Contractors appear to favour two-stage tendering, the following response from a D&B manager within a national contracting organisation being relatively typical:

'What's best for us other than negotiated is the two-stage tender process. We always ask for the cost plan to be priced, some give it you priced and some don't. We give them prelims and a programme and look at the cost plan and give them a price. We are bidding against maybe four or five at the first stage, and in the second stage there's only us, and we build it together using the best solutions within a guaranteed maximum price. That's the best scenario other than negotiated. Because nobody wants to share their ideas in that first stage, they'll put rates against a cost plan, and we'll do prelims and a programme.'

It should be noted that some contractors considered the above quote to present a fairly cold and cynical view of the two-stage tender process. Believing it to present an old-fashioned view of contractors holding a 'them and us' approach, these contractors believed an open-book approach and a culture of mutual gain should be utilised. In addition, the importance of good pre-qualification to the two-stage process was highlighted, specifically in regard to ensuring that different-sized contracting organisations are required to provide the same financial information. A common problem being that larger companies are requested to provide parent company guarantees, while smaller contracting organisations are not required to provide the same level of security.

The two-stage tendering process was found to be used in practice to demonstrate accountability in a situation where, ultimately, the client has already decided who they want to use for the scheme, as the same contractor makes clear:

'You've had a couple of meetings with the consultants, you've met the client a couple of times. I'm going from experience just recently as well, and then he says "yes we like you, we want to do this job with you, but we have got to show that we are tendering it". In return we say, "well fine, but if you turn it into a stage 2 tender process, then we can work with you in the second phase". We've worked with their consultants regularly, they know us, they like us, we like them, we'll get the best price for the client, the best design facility for the guaranteed maximum price. To a certain extent two-stage tendering is for clients who are putting their toe in the water but don't want to go down the whole partnering negotiated route.'

Single-stage 'beauty parade' tender — partially developed to pure Design and Build

The contractors develop their proposals based on the Employer's Requirements and varying levels of interaction with the client and their consultants where possible. However, in contrast to the above approach, which draws the competitive element to a close early to reduce costs, the contractors will have to develop their bid to a greater extent depending on the degree of pre-contractor scheme development. The client will then enter into a contract with the contractor submitting what the client decides is the best overall bid. The degree of pre-contractor scheme development differs, although Janssens (1991) likens a single-stage tender to a partially developed scheme, identifying the special layout, elevational treatment, that planning permission will have been sought, and a performance specification will have been used. He believes partially developed to be the most popular form of D&B, as it is perceived as offering 'the dual benefit of controlling the design, so far, yet leaving the contractor the scope to inject "buildability" and new ideas into the design development phase' (p. 41).

The selection mechanism can vary, although a multi-attribute system is required to consider the multiple dimensions that constitute the proposal and relate these to the client's project objectives. This study has found that lowest capital cost evaluation is still used for evaluating these kind of disparate proposals even where relatively large degrees of scope have been left to the contractor. This type of design competition is costly when the contractor is left with lots of scope. The client should be clear what the contractor is offering in his proposals, including the course of future development, including design and specification issues. The CIOB (1988) highlights the importance of fully documented tender submissions where the submission contains price, design, specification and programme factors. This clarifies the client's understanding of the product being offered. However, the EPSRC study found that it is seldom the case that clients receive a full set of proposals from all contractors, which affects the ability to effectively compare the tenders. This is understandable based on the time and cost implications of preparing very detailed bids allied to the probability of being awarded the contract.

Single-stage tender — detail-developed Design and Build

As mentioned in Chapter 2, the study finds that developed forms of D&B are becoming increasingly important. Here, the client is effectively using a type of risk-transferred traditional scheme; the scheme is virtually completely developed prior to contractor involvement. Questions have been raised over letting this type of scheme using a D&B contract. 'Where a project has progressed beyond the detail design stage (RIBA plan of work stage D), the design information may be too restrictive for benefit to be gained using design and build procedures and other forms of building procurement may be appropriate' (NJCC, 1995: p. 2). Contractors are not generally required to develop the design in any way as part of the tender process as is associated with other types of D&B. Although this reduces the tender resource and associated costs used in the process, the tender time allowed is often still not enough to allow adequate understanding of the detail of the scheme. The contractor needs to be able to identify risks and price appropriately.

Evaluation is generally based on the lowest capital cost and once compliance and other detailed issues are dealt with, in principle simple cost-evaluation can be used, such is the parity between bidders. However, the nature of the often-present qualifications do affect the ability to compare on simple price grounds in many instances. It should be noted that most practitioners involved in the study believed that lowest capital cost evaluation is appropriate at this stage as the quality of the contractors should have previously been assessed during the pre-qualification exercise, with an adequate benchmark of quality being met.

Establishing best-value tender mechanisms

Having previously discussed lowest cost and more wide-ranging 'best value' approaches, focus shifts to consider the direct effects on D&B tendering. The following examples are suited to one-off projects and, should the client envisage numerous schemes, the development of an integrated supply chain on a long-term basis should be considered. Negotiated approaches generally rely on open-book accounting and possibly pre-agreed profit levels with an emphasis on continually driving down costs. Study data found this type of selection provided many benefits to both clients and contractors.

Detail-developed Design and Build

Although a broad classification, the frame of reference here is schemes which have had substantial pre-contractor design and specification development. In many cases, the contractor's role is one of simply pricing the scheme, as the Employer's Requirements are so well-defined and prescriptive.

Mirroring the plethora of best practice advice, the message is to take account of non-price criteria where possible. Nevertheless, it is recognised that with developed D&B schemes, where divergence is minimal, the client often chooses to award on the basis of lowest cost. Providing the pre-qualification process is effective, and includes elements identifying the contractor's ability to add value, this type of evaluation can be used.

The ability to extract value from contractors is diminished in relation to the degree of design and specification development that takes place prior to their involvement in the scheme. The study data support the view that lowest cost evaluation is used in the majority of partially developed and developed D&B schemes. These are broad conceptual classifications and have varying Employer's Requirements development at tender stage. As stated, partially developed schemes with considerable contractor development should ideally include a multi-attribute proposal evaluation to allow consideration of the variance in the proposals.

On developed schemes, the consultants generally pre-qualify bids resulting in ranking scores for different contractors, the highest-ranking contractors being invited to tender. An understanding of the client's value system should aid in operationalising pre-qualification factors. Reference can be made to the work already completed in the field, especially Holt's (1995) detailed work on developing criteria and their attributes. Where the client has not already established an approved list, consultants' advice should be taken in developing a longlist from which a tender list of pre-qualified contractors can be developed. Pre-qualification should ideally involve an interview as part of the shortlisting process. This allows the essential personal interaction elements to be assessed and, as previously mentioned, should involve contracting staff who would be involved in the day-to-day running of the project. Following pre-qualification, the scoring of the criteria in the pre-qualification

STAGES   MAIN ACTIVITIES

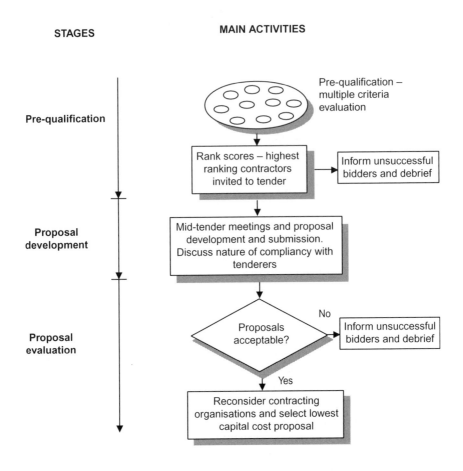

Figure 7.1. Lowest capital cost tender selection

exercise are, in most instances, only referred to when there is very little difference between bidders' costs, and it becomes a case of having to decide who can be expected to perform most proficiently. Such a type of selection is represented graphically in Figure 7.1.

CIRIA (1998) broadly classifies two different models of tendering based on whether the contractor is involved late or early. Model two is developed for the late involvement of contractors, and recognises that lowest cost may be used for selection. It also recognises the limited ability of contractors to add value at this late stage of project entry. Despite this, it attempts to increase value by focusing on:

- shortlisting contractors on the ability to add value
- evaluating the bid on whole-life costs
- taking into account aesthetics and environmental conditions.

While recognising the importance of whole-life costs, the Contractor's Proposals on such developed schemes essentially contain a price to build the scheme, any whole-life costing considerations should have previously been encapsulated in the client's scheme development. The EPSRC study detected little indication of whole-life costing being explicitly included in tenders for this developed type of D&B. The contractor, in such a situation, can only present whole-life costing implications where they have control over elements of the design and specification. Design and specification is difficult to change owing to the degree of control, for example planning permission and numerous other client-related issues, contained in Employer's Requirements. In addition, tender periods are often very short for developed D&B schemes, minimising the possibility of the contractor developing whole-life costing scenarios. Contractors also believed that there needed to be an incentive to develop expensive whole-life costings, such as shared savings.

The advice to shortlist on the ability to add value is very important. Examples of ingenuity on previous projects, specifically illustrating where the contractor was able to add value, should be sought during the pre-qualification process.

The pre-qualification scores can also be brought forward to final-award stage and combined with the price in varying proportions as part of a price/quality mechanism should the client so wish. Doing so would elevate the pre-qualification process beyond that of a simple binary controlled gate allowing contractors to tender, and is shown in Figure 7.2. This type of process explicitly relates contractor's performance potential and ability to add value to the tendered price, thus potentially minimising the problems associated with lowest-cost selection.

Partially developed and pure Design and Build

The contractor develops elements of the design to varying degrees based on the amount of development previously conducted by the client in collaboration with his consultant. As stated, partially developed schemes are sometimes evaluated simply on the basis of lowest cost. It is advised that the client team evaluate the Contractor's Proposals, taking account of the contractor's design, in contrast to a simple cost-evaluation at this stage.

STAGES   MAIN ACTIVITIES

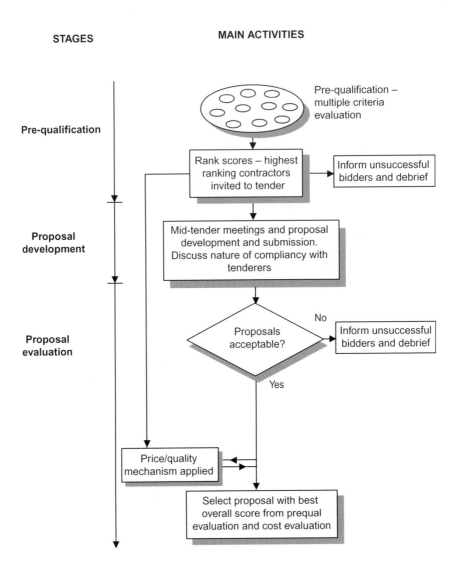

Figure 7.2. Price/quality mechanism based on pre-qualification score evaluation

Simply evaluating on the basis of cost where there is design variance in wider factors than simply capital cost is a limiting exercise. The contractors involved need to be pre-qualified as in detail-developed D&B above, taking account of both project-specific and general criteria.

Following qualification, certain contractors are invited to tender, and should be furnished with the Employer's Requirements document. Just as with developed forms of D&B, the client can choose various selection mechanisms.

The client's value system, as developed through the value-management exercise, needs to be expressed in a hierarchy, with weights attached to each criteria and sub-criteria as seen fit. This information should be fully expressed in the tender documents, i.e. the tree's sub-criteria should be expressed. The client would be well served by employing a professional to manage the tender process, ideally an expert in tendering, who was previously involved in the value-management workshops. This individual should be the first point of contact for tendering contractors, and can manage tender enquiries, hopefully reducing transfusion between contractors as they access the client team. The time available to contractors to interact with the client and his consultants during the tender process needs managing, with equity and impartiality being practised throughout. Even though the client may not be aware of the technical nature of the scheme, their input is important to gauge the scheme's relationship to their value system. Consultants involved in the project, specifically the tender specialist, will be able to clarify technical elements, including questioning the contractor. The tender specialist needs to exhibit the following qualities:

- be proactive and decisive
- have the ability to consider issues and propose solutions
- be able to take the initiative
- have a thorough understanding of the client's value system, including wider business objectives.

There are generally two strands of evaluation — documentary and presentation, with the documentary analysis being conducted in the first instance. The client needs to decide in advance whether the price and non-price elements of the bid will be evaluated in isolation to avoid price dominating the exercise. There are two main ways of dealing with different proposals, as outlined below.

Multi-attribute ranking of proposal

This describes a process aimed at maintaining the evaluation of the different proposals' relative strengths and weaknesses until the final evaluation stage, where price and non-price criteria are amalgamated in an overall score. The proposals are evaluated in conjunction with the client's objectives as operationalised in the value-tree output from the value-

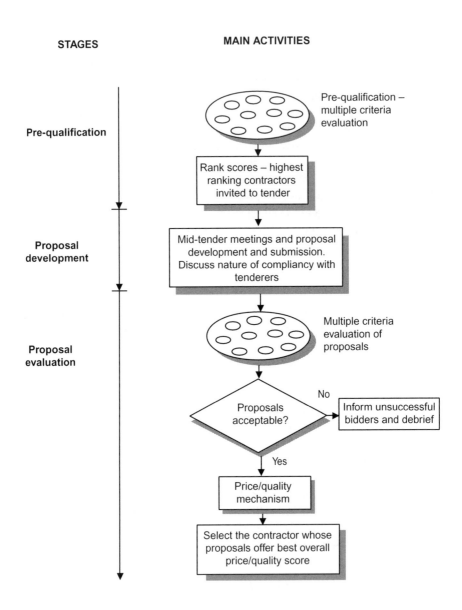

STAGES   MAIN ACTIVITIES

Pre-qualification

Pre-qualification –
multiple criteria
evaluation

Rank scores – highest
ranking contractors
invited to tender

Proposal
development

Mid-tender meetings and proposal
development and submission.
Discuss nature of compliancy with
tenderers

Proposal
evaluation

Multiple criteria
evaluation of
proposals

Proposals
acceptable?

No → Inform unsuccessful
bidders and debrief

Yes

Price/quality
mechanism

Select the contractor whose
proposals offer best overall
price/quality score

Figure 7.3. Multi-attribute price/quality evaluation based on proposal score

management exercise. Ideally, a whole-life costing exercise should form part of this evaluation process. A general outline of this approach is shown in Figure 7.3.

Multi-attribute threshold score

This process is subtly different to that described above and underpins the case-study example. Following pre-qualification, proposals are evaluated by taking account of various criteria, as shown above. However, proposals are rated and, providing they meet a certain threshold for different criteria, the lowest cost bid is selected. The threshold level is developed based on the client's objectives. Schemes are grouped as responsive in a similar way to the pass/fail binary decision used in parts of the pre-qualification process. The responsive schemes are then generally evaluated on lowest capital cost, although whole-life costs can be taken into account. Using this method, the differentiation in the proposals is not ultimately taken into account in the final evaluation. Where responsive schemes are very close to each other, the non-price evaluation scores may be used to sensitise the selection.

Scheme development issues

The previously presented continuum is based on the amount of pre-contractor design and specification development. Throughout this book, the EPSRC research has added support to the assertion that limiting the contractor's flexibility in meeting the client's needs, ultimately limits the ability to add value and make best use of the contractor's construction experience. Clients may have a clear idea of how much control they wish to exert over their projects, and the extent to which they wish to limit contractor input. This may have been informed by previous experience, talking to other clients, taking their consultant's advice, or indeed the contractor's advice. Clients surveyed chose the following as their first point of contact on D&B schemes: architect (38·2%), contractor (26·5%), quantity surveyor (14·7%). The data support the view that many architects advise their clients to develop the scheme as far as possible prior to contractor involvement in order to minimise the 'quality reduction' effect that architects perceive contractors to have. An architect provided the following response when asked for possible improvements to D&B:

'I think the further one can go before you tie yourself down to D&B the better. If the client is really keen on the advantages of D&B, then you will certainly try and push him down to not going out to tender until you've done stage E for example or G, but that allows more to be done than a performance specification, unless he's just doing a simple shed. I mean we would really try and urge him away from it at stage C because we think it foolish.'

Many contractors interviewed disagreed with the logic of the above argument, yet agreed that what they regarded as a 'backward view' was still held by some architects. These kind of arguments are common today and, are not, as would ideally be the case, a relic of the power and authority arguments that characterised early D&B practice. Architects may have lost their traditional role as leader in some projects, but interviews suggest that those who perceive D&B as a business opportunity and not as a reason to adopt a defensive position are perceived favourably by the client. Wherever possible, contractors advise clients to liase directly with them, taking advantage of their advanced planning skills, thereby avoiding what they see as the disruptive influence of the architect who is invariably predisposed to more of a conventional form of tendering and the control that this brings. Industry advice is clear on the need to involve the contractor early in the project, whether through negotiation or competition. This book concurs with this advice in encouraging clients, even those who may unfortunately have previously suffered at the hands of unscrupulous contractors, to allow contractors early entry to the project. This is not a call to award contracts on the basis of poorly defined specifications, designs and contractual issues. The contractor should be involved early following rigorous pre-qualification, with the actual contract award most appropriately carried out when the scheme is relatively well-developed, and all sides are clear about risk and responsibility. The key is to choose the best overall project team and not simply concentrate on the identification of one party to rely on.

Output requirements

Defining the scheme in terms of the outputs required is currently considered the most advantageous technique by major authors in the field. Fredrickson (1998) makes clear the relationship between information and assumption, where the less information provided results in more assumptions being made by the contractor and, hence, greater differentiation between proposed schemes. Assumptions are best tested by dialogue between the client and contractor, although transfusion, as already explained, should be limited. Risk registers are important to increase the understanding and allocation of risks, minimising potential future problems. The client's attitude to risk is also important and many new procurement initiatives render the client a stakeholder in the project-delivery framework, thus negating simple risk transfer. The client's objectives should be used to operationalise selection criteria and develop a specification that is clearly balanced in the favour of output requirements. The need to make the client's objectives clear and detailed should never be confused with making the project overly controlling.

> As additional design development documentation is prepared, the bidders will have less flexibility. If the client does not want to allow any bidding flexibility, the project might be best delivered using a conventional process.
>
> (Fredrickson, 1998: p. 78)

The importance of involving the contractor early in projects has been reinforced by many in the industry over the years. Hill (2000) believes contractors should be involved:

> As soon as possible . . . Sophisticated clients bring their main contractor and strategic suppliers on-board as soon as the scope of the project is defined. They then work together with the client's professional advisers to develop fully the functional brief, conceptual solutions and the cost plan. The most important principle of early involvement is avoiding uncertainty. Uncertainty costs money.
>
> (p. 3)

Our study has shown that the advantages of involving the contractor early are not being utilised by many in industry. Ideally this means utilising the experience of a balanced project team to produce a product benefiting from a multi-facetted approach. Risk and responsibility can be properly identified and ascribed prior to a commitment to build.

The time allowed for contractor scheme development

The majority of contractors involved in the study complained that there is never enough time allowed at the tender stage. Many consultants similarly acknowledge that contractors are not given enough time to develop their bids. A consultant working within a client department gave the following response:

> 'Never long enough. You never do, do you? Four, five weeks is not long enough. I've been told that this week actually.'

However, clients who wish to minimise the pre-construction phases to as short a period as possible often dictate the periods to consultants. Contractors will often request an extension to the tender period, although many stated that unless all the contractors request an extension they are rarely given. Additionally, should an extension be granted, it is often only 50% of that requested, which is an interesting finding when one considers the acknowledgement that time frames are often not sufficient.

The varying degrees of pre-contractor design and specification development in D&B obviously affects the time needed to prepare tenders. It is generally advised that contractors in detail-developed D&B be given less time than pure D&B. This is understandable as the contractor does not have to undertake the scheme development work that constitutes a pure D&B competitive bid. However, our data show that contractors are generally given four weeks to prepare their bids on developed D&B; the same tender period as typically allowed for tendering on traditional projects. This time is clearly not sufficient, as contractors need to become acquainted with the scheme, prepare a bill of quantities, and understand the risks involved as the nature of risk transfer is more onerous in D&B than in traditional arrangements. The CIB (1997) recognises this in advising a minimum of 12 weeks for D&B tenders as opposed to a minimum of eight weeks for traditional contracting. Contractors rely heavily on sub-contractors and consultants during the tender development phase, whether for pricing or more complex design development issues.

The importance of the contractor's tender management skills cannot be overstressed. Our data highlight typical problems associated with poor management of the tender process, including sub-contractors being given partial information on which to produce estimates, and a last-minute philosophy as an employers agent comments:

'What really does annoy you of course is that for the first four weeks you hear nothing. Then for the last week you are running round like a headless chicken taking contractors round site. I mean the normal story is that the estimator gets it on his desk, for two weeks he does nothing, it's a standard story throughout the industry. Then he might pick it up and read it, then he puts it back down again because he's got other things to do.'

It is this 'last minute' mentality that the client's consultants blame for the way that sub-contractors are often given only part of the information they need to provide a package price to contractors. However, contractors contest this, and argue that such views do not take account of the reality that the first few weeks of the tender period involve such processes as the development of the bill of quantities. In addition, contractors argue that the client's consultants often provide them with late scheme information, thus increasing time pressure in the tender period. The client's belief that tender times are currently sufficient is borne out by the research study data — 91·4% of clients believe that contractors have enough time to tender for the project. There would appear to be an element of divergence between consultants' and clients' thoughts on this matter. Consultants employed by the client have stated that, in certain circumstances, the nature of scheme development is so great that contractors need extra time to fully comprehend the detail of the scheme; time that is not allowed. This view is reflected in the statistical data, which show that 37·8% of consultants do not believe contractors generally have sufficient time to tender. It may be that in some circumstances consultants have difficulty in making it clear to clients the complexity and scope of the tender-development process. For many clients, the old adage 'time is money' overrides a more balanced view of the situation, thus increasing pressures on the contractors. We advise a general increase in tender periods, specifically for the popular developed forms, which should ideally be given at least a six-week period, instead of the often encountered four week time-frame. In addition, the dates for release of information need planning to allow resource usage to be arranged.

Feedback and debrief

Providing contractors with the reasons for their lack of success should theoretically allow them to be more successful in their next tendering opportunity. The principle is similar to that employed in performance measurement; that an objective review of various aspects of current performance can facilitate future improvements by focusing efforts where they are most needed. HM Treasury Central Unit on Procurement (CUP) Guidance Note 56 (1997) believes the benefits of a debrief to be threefold.

1. Increasing the potential for improved value for money on future orders.
2. Assisting suppliers to be more successful in wider markets.
3. Gaining more information on the marketplace, in general, and supplier specialisation in particular.

In addition to providing contractors with the potential for increased success in future projects, it can foster a sense of closure and be seen as a type of return for the tendering resources unsuccessfully employed. Debrief should ideally be used following both pre-qualification and tender evaluation, although the cost of both exercises should be considered in relation to the project size. The nature of the debrief should reflect the type of selection process utilised. For example, very well-developed schemes that have simply employed price criteria following qualification are relatively straightforward and typically include cost information showing relative positions with other competing contractors. Where a multi-attribute evaluation has taken place, the actual scores given, and reasons behind them, should be clearly communicated. Feedback can take a documentary form, or this can be augmented with a debrief meeting to gain a deeper understanding of the evaluation.

Some proactive contractors, who are actually awarded the contract, conduct their own project-evaluation exercises with the client. A contractor explains in his own words what such an exercise comprises:

> 'We do have our own internal re-examination, and we do customer service questionnaires. We do one in the middle of the job with the client to see how we are getting on and see if we can address matters during a course of a job. Then we also do a "close-out" meeting at the end of a job with a customer service questionnaire just to see how they got on with us on that. If we are not interrogated at the end of a job then we certainly promote that interrogation of ourselves anyway. We ask questions and let them tell us what's wrong, we don't try and defend ourselves, even if what they say is inaccurate, we literally want to hear what their perceptions are of our performance. We've developed it ourselves, we get a score out of ten for every job and the idea is to kick that as high as we possibly can.'

This example shows how useful the client's perceptions of contractor performance are to the contractor. Just as performance in delivery of the project is important to contractors, so too is performance in tendering.

Value management based multi-attribute approach

As stated in Chapter 5, value-management workshops may be undertaken at various stages of a construction project. The titles given to these stages vary in different publications. Sometimes the design phase, which is often referenced to the RIBA 'Plan of work' is used to describe these stages. In other publications, the processes within the value-management exercises are used to title the stage or workshop. For example, information, creative, evaluation, development and presentation phases provide a standardised framework referred to as the 'job plan'. While this can lead to confusion, the title given to workshops is more an academic issue, and secondary to the quality of the activities undertaken. Value-management techniques should be individually developed in accordance with the needs and resources of each particular client. Nevertheless, there are key points in D&B projects when value-management exercises are more valuable, which are outlined below.

The pre-brief or initial workshop

At the very initial stages a pre-brief or initial workshop should be held. At this point the team is gathering and discussing the most basic information regarding the client's business case. It may be determined that a construction project is not the best solution to the client's needs; renting existing space may be more appropriate. However, if construction is considered an option, the client's priorities should be considered carefully and the various procurement options evaluated. There is an overlap between what can probably be described as traditional briefing and value management. Although the terms 'value management' and 'briefing' have specific meanings, they should not be seen as covering mutually exclusive activities. Individual meetings will almost definitely precede the initial workshop. However, a formal workshop at an early stage, with a wider group of stakeholders, has many advantages. This is because it is at this point that the client's value system sets a template for the remainder of the project. Limitations in the communication of this value system can only reduce the likelihood of a best-value solution.

The brief development workshop

Following the decision to build, made during the information gathering stage, a second workshop should be held to develop the initial strategic brief into a more detailed performance specification (Kelly and Male, 2002). During this meeting, or series of meetings, a carefully structured set of activities should be planned in order to fully elicit and develop the client's needs. These discussions will then form the basis for the development of the client's requirements in addition to assessment criteria used in D&B tender evaluation. Techniques such as lateral thinking are often used to assist in the development of ideas; this is often described as the creative phase in value-management literature. In D&B

projects the ideas should ideally be less focused on providing design solutions than in traditional procurement projects. Nevertheless, this depends on the degree of pre-contract design and specification development intended by the client. In order to develop tender evaluation criteria, the simple multi-attribute rating technique (SMART) (Green, 1992) is ideal. In this context, the aim of the technique is to structure the client's value system through a weighted value-tree. This can then be used as a scoring mechanism to evaluate contractors' proposals.

As an alternative to the above two-stage approach, a single-stage, or 'charette', workshop may be employed. This single-stage activity would be undertaken after the development of a brief and would act as a review mechanism. Although this approach is common in the UK, there is a danger that the brief has already been set and a better encapsulation of the client's value system may therefore be more difficult to elicit. The following example is developed from the work of Green (1992) and a value-management workshop undertaken as part of the EPSRC project to develop criteria for a community learning centre. It is included to demonstrate how a value-management workshop can result in a weighted hierarchy, which can be used in the D&B tender evaluation.

Developing a weighted hierarchy using the SMART technique

The stages described below should be distributed between the various value-management workshops and a tender-evaluation meeting. For example, during the pre-brief workshop, stages 1 to 3, or 1 to 4, may be undertaken. These earlier stages should ideally then be reviewed before undertaking the later stages in the second workshop. An alternative would be to complete all the stages, with the exception of stage 6, during a single workshop. However, the resources available and the nature of the client organisation will determine how the following stages are adapted and integrated within the procurement process.

Stage 1 — An introduction to the process

It is essential that all participants feel a sense of ownership of the process if it is to be successful in articulating the client's value system. Many of the participants in a workshop, for example building users, will be completely unfamiliar with the nature of the briefing process and could easily be alienated by terms such as 'value management'. Therefore, the initial stage should be used to educate all those involved in the process.

The facilitator should explain, in very simple language, the processes involved and the end result; this being that participants will have an opportunity to impact on the final project constructed. This should increase the enthusiasm for the workshop and confirm to group members that they are valuable contributors to the finished project. It is suggested that an example project, which is not too similar to the actual project, is used to demonstrate to the group the various stages of the procurement process and the value-management exercise. If a very similar project is used it may quash creativity in the brainstorming sessions because a 'solution' may appear to be readily recommended by the facilitator; something that must be avoided. Certain ground rules need establishing to stimulate participation. For example, higher-level and lower-level staff may be involved, and to avoid inhibiting the full involvement of lower-level staff they should be assured that their comments in the workshop will not lead to repercussions outside its boundaries.

Stage 2 — Generation of scheme objectives

The aim of this stage is to determine how different stakeholders view the objectives of the project. Brainstorming can be helpful for developing ideas in this process. The end result of this stage is likely to be a large list of unstructured objectives that can then be organised into the key design objectives of the project.

In the case study undertaken, participants were asked to consider the question, 'what would make an *excellent* community learning centre?'. Stakeholders representing the city council, community groups and centre staff worked in small groups and brainstormed the question, recording their thoughts on paper. These were then used as a focus for a more structured group discussion to bring ideas together. The following list represents only a small part of the output from stage 2.

What would make an *excellent* community learning centre?

- Good security
- Canteen
- Lockers for staff
- Comfortable meeting rooms
- Easy to clean and maintain
- Vandalism protection
- Generally appealing to users
- CCTV
- Useful for a range of community initiatives
- Disabled access.

This list illustrates that 'opening up' the client's value system has produced an interesting mix of design objectives and basic design-solutions. For example, 'good security' can be encompassed in various design approaches, whereas 'CCTV' is perceived as part of the solution to this objective. The objectives themselves are also set at different levels. For example, 'useful for a range of community initiatives' may include as a sub-objective 'good meeting rooms'. Stage 2 should ideally be as open and creative as possible, while it is the aim of stage 4 to rationalise and prioritise these objectives into a meaningful format.

Stage 3 — Instruction on how to create a value tree

There are significant dangers if participants are asked to construct a value tree immediately after the brainstorming discussion. Participants must not feel overwhelmed as this may lead to them feeling disenfranchised by the process. This may happen if they do not understand what they are asked to do, or alternatively if the process is dominated by the facilitator. Therefore, it is suggested at this stage that the alternative project type introduced at stage 1, say for example a hospital, is used by the facilitator to demonstrate how to construct and then weight a value tree. This should be undertaken slowly with appropriate teaching materials.

Stage 4 — Participants construct a value tree

The end result of this session should be a measurable list of objectives that can be used to evaluate alternative contractors' design proposals. Participants need to return to the brainstorming discussion output and attempt to rationalise this list into a manageable hierarchy of objectives. The facilitator should assist in the process by explaining how various objectives may be combined or split into sub-objectives to produce a sound balance that will be useable at tender stage.

In the community learning centre case-study, participants engaged in prolonged debate to reduce the highest order objectives down to four. These were:

- a welcoming atmosphere for all
- an efficient facility
- a community landmark
- an attractive work environment for staff.

There are a number of ways in which the value tree could have been organised, it is important to recognise that there is no theoretical optimal solution. However, the thought and communication processes promoted by such workshops uncover a more detailed and representative picture of a client's value system than traditional briefing.

Stage 5 — Participants weight the value tree

All the objectives are not of equal importance and the weighting of the value tree allows this to be considered in the evaluation of solutions. It should be noted that the weighting of the tree may occur at stage 4; in parallel with the tree construction. However, in the community learning centre case-study it was found that, although rank order in the tree may be considered initially, a period of reflection prior to formal weighting is beneficial. Therefore, if two workshops are being used, a review of the value tree and the weighting priorities could form the focus of the work in the second workshop. If this is the case, it may be appropriate for the facilitator to review the process of weighting with a worked example.

To weight the value tree each level should be considered separately and each set of branches should equate to 1. For example, in the case study, the participants ranked the four highest-level objectives as illustrated in Table 7.1.

The lowest of these objectives, 'a community landmark', is then given a weight of 10. The score attributed to the second lowest was then given a higher score which represents its relative importance. So, for example, if 'an efficient facility' were considered to be twice as important as the lowest objective, a score of 20 would be applied. These scores are then normalised to equal unity, as shown in Table 7.2.

The weights chosen obviously have a dramatic impact on the relative importance of the score received by each design solution for each criteria associated with the design. Therefore, careful consideration and

Table 7.1. Highest order objectives

Rank	Objective
1	A welcoming atmosphere for all
2	An attractive work environment for staff
3	An efficient facility
4	A community landmark

Table 7.2. Normalised weighted objectives

Rank	Objective	Weight	Normalised weight
1	A welcoming atmosphere for all	50	50/125=0·40
2	An attractive work environment for staff	35	0·28
3	An efficient facility	30	0·24
4	A community landmark	10	0·08
	Total	125	1·00

discussion are required at this stage, particularly if the tendering contractors are to be made aware of the weighting scheme, as is advised. In the community learning centre case-study, some of the lower-order 'twigs' (or sub-criteria) could have been equally applied to alternative higher-order branches, but are included only under one branch for simplicity. For example, a 'safe and secure design' was important to both centre users and workers. This should be accounted for in the weighting, chosen to ensure its final score reflects its true importance. It should be noted that the objectives developed during the value-management process should also form a focus for the client's consultants to use in the development of the Employer's Requirements.

Figure 7.4 is the final weighted value-tree for the community learning centre example and illustrates how the final weights are achieved by multiplying through each branch.

Stage 6 — Contractor design proposals evaluated against value tree

This is the final stage of the analysis and may be performed in a variety of ways. The ultimate aim is to identify the contractor's proposals that provide the best overall solution for a particular client. It should be noted that, although the process results in a numerical score, this should not be seen as an 'answer', which is simplistically used to select a contractor. Rather, this should be seen as an aid to the professional decision-making process. Before the final value score can be calculated, the relative importance of cost and quality needs to be established, as shown later. For example, if both were considered to be of the same importance, a ratio of 50:50 would be used. In the community learning centre example, costs are weighted at 70 and quality at 30. Here we are using the term 'quality' in its

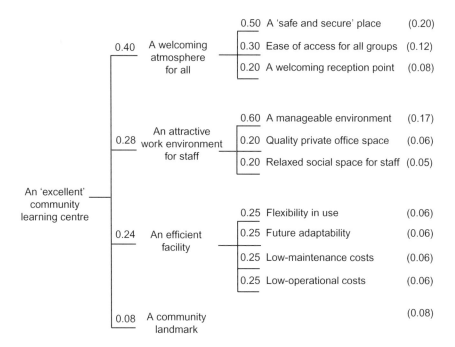

Figure 7.4. Weighted value-tree

broadest sense. It should also be taken into account that some of the criteria include scores for lifecycle costs. If a full lifecycle-costing analysis was undertaken on the whole project, then it is also possible to include the results with the capital costs on the cost side of the equation. However, in the example the lifecycle-costing results are converted to a score on the quality side of the equation.

Each should be dealt with in turn and carefully compared with the criteria established in the value tree. Scores should be given within a range between 0 and 100 for each criteria. It is accepted that this process is largely subjective and members of the evaluation team may disagree. However, the success of the final project will also be subjective, so this should not preclude evaluation. If objective analysis is possible, for example on operating costs, the figures provided by the contractors should be converted to a score ranging from 0–100. One possibility is to give the lowest operating cost a value of 100 and then reduce the other designs by a percentage equivalent to the percentage above the lowest.

Table 7.3 illustrates the case-study example of the community learning centre. Three contractors' proposals are evaluated against the weighted

Table 7.3. *Value management multi-attribute evaluation matrix*

Assessment criteria	Weighting	Tender A		Tender B		Tender C	
		Score	Weighted score	Score	Weighted score	Score	Weighted score
A safe and secure place	0·20	70	14·0	50	10·0	75	15·0
Ease of access for all groups	0·12	60	7·2	50	6·0	65	7·8
A welcoming reception point	0·08	20	1·6	20	1·6	70	5·6
A manageable environment	0·17	50	8·5	30	5·1	60	10·2
Quality private-office space	0·06	70	4·2	50	3·0	60	3·6
Relaxed social space for staff	0·05	80	4·0	20	1·0	85	4·25
Flexibility in use	0·06	60	3·6	40	2·4	75	4·5
Future adaptability	0·06	70	4·2	35	2·1	70	4·2
Low-maintenance costs	0·06	80	4·8	40	2·4	70	4·2
Low-operational costs	0·06	80	4·8	40	2·4	40	2·4
A community landmark	0·08	60	4·8	30	2·4	80	6·4
Total quality score			**61·7**		**38·4**		**68·2**

Table 7.4. Tender price score mechanism

Tender	Tender sum	Percentage above lowest	Price score
A	£4 387 000	7	93
B	£4 100 000	0	100
C	£5 535 000	35	65

criteria derived from the value tree in a matrix format. The matrix illustrates that, excluding capital costs, the best design solution is tender C. Care should be taken in the selection of the tender evaluation panel. Although it may not be easy for groups of people without specialist knowledge to interpret drawings, it is essential that the analysis be carried out in the same spirit as the original value-tree development, with the same people being involved in both exercises.

Following the establishment of the final quality score, it is then necessary to score the relative prices. The tender figures for the community centre example are illustrated in Table 7.4. The lowest tender is given a score of 100 and then more expensive proposals are scored relatively lower.

The final stage is to compare the relative scores for quality and price. This results in a final score, which may be thought of as an overall final value score (FVS), the calculation of which is illustrated in Table 7.5.

Table 7.5. Final price/quality tender analysis matrix

Tender	Price score	Price weighting	Weighted price score (WPS)	Quality score	Quality weighting	Weighted quality score (WQS)	(WPS) + (WQS) = FVS
A	93	0·7	65·1	61·7	0·3	18·5	83·6
B	100	0·7	70·0	38·4	0·3	11·5	81·5
C	65	0·7	45·5	68·2	0·3	20·5	66·0

The above example illustrates the different decisions that would be made depending on the selection procedure. For example, if the lowest price were used tender B would be selected, had the highest quality tender been used tender C would be selected, while tender A would be selected had a combination of price and quality been used. Although the client is ultimately still able to choose any of the tenders, the use of value-management workshops and techniques allows a more thorough examination of the objectives of the project. This, in turn, facilitates a more structured comparison of Contractor's Proposals against those objectives, resulting in a more holistic informed selection.

Other price/quality mechanisms

In the above example, the final value score was computed by equating price and quality criteria. The price score was calculated by assigning the lowest capital cost a base score of 100 and adjusting others in relation to this. Alternative price-quality approaches have been published, such as the price discounting model by CIRIA (1998). CIRIA present two models, one essentially the same as that used in the value-management approach above and the other termed the 'price-discounting model'. However, it should be noted that clients involved in the EPSRC study found it less transparent, as they were confused by the incorporation of quality scores with the tender price.

Lifecycle costing

This section outlines the use of lifecycle-costing techniques with specific reference to their use in the tender evaluation exercise in D&B projects. The section begins by establishing a rationale for the use of lifecycle costing, followed by a description of the basic principles and a worked example. Finally, some practical considerations are outlined.

Rationale for lifecycle costing in Design and Build tender evaluation

When attempting to establish best value in construction projects, it has long been recognised that initial capital cost is only part of the equation.

Costs are incurred throughout the life of a building and this information is required for effective decision-making. The process of analysing these costs is generally termed 'lifecycle costing'. However, there are currently a number of similar terms used within publications such as whole-life and through-life costs (Pasquire and Swaffield, 2002). The Royal Institution of Chartered Surveyors (RICS) defines lifecycle costs as 'the present value of the total cost of an asset over its operating life, including capital cost, occupation costs, operating costs and the cost of benefit or the eventual disposal of the asset at the end of its life' (RICS, 1999: p. 1). The above definition, in simple terms, means all the costs associated with a building asset over its lifetime, and will probably correspond with practitioners' understanding, and is therefore adopted in this book.

Lifecycle-costing techniques have long been utilised in industries outside the construction sector. For example, fleet managers in the motor industry typically consider costs of fuel, servicing and repair in addition to initial purchase price and disposal value of vehicles. Even members of the public are unlikely to consider purchasing a vehicle without reference to the operating costs of particular models. In general terms, all the costs of purchasing any form of capital asset need careful consideration if a well-informed decision is to be made.

In the construction industry, the forecasting of costs over extensive time frames is necessary if client satisfaction is to be maximised. Lifecycle costing should be thought of as a *decision-informing* tool that can be used at various points in the procurement of a project. At the inception stage, decisions have the greatest impact on the future design and management of the project. Therefore, in D&B projects the principal advisor should clearly communicate the long-term financial implications of various broad design alternatives. The client should also understand that the accuracy of data at this early stage is poor and will only improve as further details are determined. It maybe that during the briefing process the lifecycle-costing information provided illustrates that construction work would not best meet the client's business case and an alternative, for example leasing existing space, may be more appropriate. If a decision is made to proceed with the construction project following the briefing stage, the pre-tender design develops to a point dependent on the form of D&B being used. For example, on a developed form of D&B, the client's professional team could produce detailed lifecycle-costing options. This information would then be used to determine design options, for example types of window, and the final decision included as a specification item in the Employers' Requirements. However, if a more pure form of D&B is considered appropriate, a requirement for a lifecycle-costing exercise could be requested in the Contractors' Proposals in response to performance specifications contained in the Employer's Requirements. For example, the contractors could be asked to provide information on the maintenance and fuel consumption costs of alternative heating systems that fulfil the performance requirements over a 20-year period. However, it should be noted that this information is often not easily available, although its importance is fuelling its development.

It is therefore possible to see that lifecycle costing is a technique that can assist the decision-making process at various stages in the procurement process. As stated, in D&B the parties undertaking the majority of analysis will depend on the form of D&B being used. The extent of lifecycle costing undertaken will depend on the characteristics of the project and the nature of the client's business case. However, where possible the technique should be used to inform professional judgement and enhance advice to clients.

The basic principles

Before illustrating further the development of a lifecycle-costing exercise, it is necessary to explore some of the key concepts surrounding the process.

The study period

When undertaking a lifecycle-costing analysis, it is necessary to establish the forecasting time-frame under consideration, which is described as the 'study period'. The life of a building may exceed several hundred years and because the risk associated with the forecasting costs is directly proportional to the length of time under consideration, a study period of less than the physical life of the building is normally used. Buildings are capital assets and development occurs in direct response to either a business, personal or social need. However, over time these needs change and alternative uses for the land resources take precedence. The period of time over which the current use of the land resources is most profitable is known as the economic life of the building. This is typically shorter than the physical life. As illustrated in Figure 7.5, the economic life of the building can be understood as ending when the value of the next best alternative land use, less the costs of redevelopment, exceeds the value of the current use.

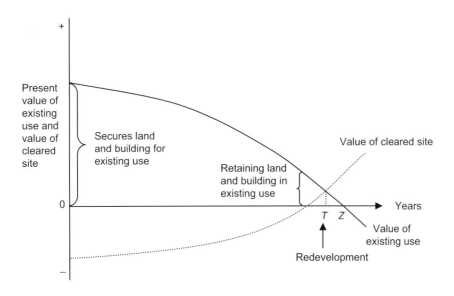

Figure 7.5. The timing of redevelopment (adapted from Harvey, 1996)

When developing a comprehensive lifecycle-costing analysis of several scheme designs, the study period may equate with the economic life of the building. However, if lifecycle costing is being used in a more specific manner, for example to examine the relative costs of two alternative heating designs over 20 years, it may be more appropriate if the study period is significantly shorter than the overall economic life of the building. The study period is mainly dependent on the purpose of the lifecycle costing exercise and the risk associated with the accuracy of the forecasting data.

Two further terms often discussed in relation to lifecycle costing are 'deterioration' and 'obsolescence'. Ashworth and Hogg (2000) distinguish between the two terms, stating that deterioration is controlled, planned and able to be forecasted. Obsolescence, on the other hand, is more difficult to predict and control because it is related to a large number of factors, which may be technological, functional, economic, social, legal or aesthetic. This illustrates that, in common with many other areas of surveying, terms are not consistently applied across the field of literature. The terms 'deterioration' and 'obsolescence' can be broadly thought of as analogous to the physical and economic life of a building.

Costs associated with lifecycle-costing analysis

There is a range of costs associated with the production of a lifecycle-costing analysis. The first of these are typically referred to as the initial capital cost or initial investment costs. If a full lifecycle-costing analysis is being undertaken, these costs comprise the tender sum for the project and various associated fees, for example professional advisor fees. However, as stated above, lifecycle costing is a decision-making tool and it may not be appropriate to undertake a full analysis. Therefore, only the initial capital sum of the components under consideration may be included in the analysis. The initial costs are often taken as occurring at one point in time, usually the present, and hence there is less risk associated with the forecast of these sums.

Future costs also need to be forecasted in lifecycle costing and these may be grouped in various ways. First, operations costs need to be calculated. These typically relate to energy consumption throughout the study period and are normally discounted on an annual basis. Second, maintenance costs need to be taken into account. These are scheduled activities that can be planned based on current construction knowledge. For example, manufacturers typically specify maintenance activities for the expected life of their boiler products. Third, repair and unscheduled replacement costs need to be considered. These are unplanned activities and, hence, are more difficult to predict than operations and maintenance costs. For example, vandalism at a school may require the replacement of doors before the end of the planned life. Professional judgement and experience of both construction technology and the wider context of the project are important in reducing the risk associated with the forecasting of such repair costs. Finally, it may be appropriate to estimate a salvage value and demolition costs, although in practice, owing to the long timescales involved, this is often omitted.

The discounting process

The process of discounting is fundamental to lifecycle-costing calculations. This is because money received or expended at different points in time cannot be directly compared. £10 today is not worth the same as £10 in 20 years' time. This is known as the 'time value of money'. Therefore, in order that all future costs can be compared, a process known as 'discounting' is applied to normalise all costs to one point in time. The methods employed to discount cash flows to the present value are very simple to apply. However, considerable professional judgement is required in the selection of the variables necessary for the calculations, for example the choice of discount rate.

Calculations utilising discounted cash flows are now normally performed on bespoke computer programs or spreadsheets. However, it is useful to understand and reflect on the process of discounting before inputting assumptions into a computer to avoid what is often termed 'black box' syndrome. In this context, this occurs when calculation results become difficult to interpret and communicate to clients, as the practitioner fails to fully understand the process that led to the results. The following examples will briefly outline compound interest, present value and net present value, these being the most commonly used concepts in lifecycle costing.

Compound interest factors
The compound interest factors, sometimes termed the 'amount of £1', are used to determine what the sum of £1 will accumulate to over a given number of years at a given interest rate. It is simply a matter of multiplying the initial sum by the interest factor, where i is the interest rate and n equals the number of years as shown below.

$$(1+i)^n$$

For example, £700 placed on deposit at an interest rate of 6% for 12 years is calculated as in the following example.

$$£700 \times (1 \cdot 06)^{12} = £1408$$

Present value factors
Where a future amount of money needs to be discounted to the present value, a *present value* factor is used. This works in the opposite direction to the compound interest factors, as previously demonstrated above. The general equation used is:

$$\frac{1}{(1+i)^n} \quad \text{or} \quad (1+i)^{-n}$$

Hence, taking the previous example of £700 growing to £1408, £1408 in 12 years, discounted at an annual rate of 6%, should equal £700.

$$£1408 \times (1 \cdot 06)^{-12} = £700$$

The use of present value factors is very common in lifecycle costing owing to the need to compare future forecasted costs. Computer spreadsheets offer a very convenient way to calculate these costs. For example, to compute the above discounting factor using Microsoft Excel the following formula can be used:

=(1.06)^-12

Present value of £1 per annum
It is often the case in lifecycle-costing calculations that operational costs, such as fuel, occur regularly and, as such, are normally discounted at the end of each year of the study period. As an alternative to calculating a separate present value for each year of a recurring cost, it is often more convenient to calculate the present value of £1 per annum.

Present value factors:

$$= \frac{1}{(1+i)^n}$$

Present value of £1 per annum:

$$= \frac{1}{1+i} + \frac{1}{(1+i)^2} + \frac{1}{(1+i)^3} \cdots \frac{1}{(1+i)^n}$$

$$= \frac{1 - \dfrac{1}{(1+i)^n}}{i} \quad \text{or} \quad = \frac{1-(1+i)^{-n}}{i}$$

For example, a cost of £100 per annum for 20 years discounted at 8% equates to:

$$= \frac{1 - \dfrac{1}{(1\cdot08)^{20}}}{0\cdot08}$$

$$= £100 \times 9\cdot818$$

$$= £981\cdot80$$

As an example, say the annual fuel costs for a boiler were £1000 per annum for the next 20 years, the present value of this cost at a rate of 8% could be calculated as:

$9 \cdot 818 \times 1000 = £9818$

This demonstrates how simple equations can take account of the time value of money. The discount rate and study period are critical variables, therefore, when asking contractors to include lifecycle-costing analysis, clients should make these parameters clear.

Practical considerations

The mathematics of lifecycle costing are straightforward and even comprehensive project-wide analysis can be routinely performed using a computer spreadsheet. However, there are a number of practical considerations that can make the integration of lifecycle costing in the overall tender-evaluation problematic.

Discount rate decisions

As previously stated, the selection of the discount rate requires careful consideration. The discount rate chosen should reflect the client's time value of money. This means the amount by which clients value immediate consumption in preference to deferred or postponed consumption (Bannock *et al.*, 1998). When lifecycle-costing exercises are included in tenders, it is necessary to inform the contractors of the discount rate to use. This ensures that all the tenders are assessed on an equal basis. However, the data from our research suggest that in several projects contractors were not informed of the discount rate to use. Indeed, many contractors complained that clients often requested lifecycle-costing information to be provided, but they believed that neither they nor their consultants adequately understood what was being asked for and what to do with the information once provided.

The client's principal advisor should establish, through consultation with the client, an appropriate discount rate which reflects such issues as the cost of borrowing money and the client's attitude to risk. It should also be made clear whether real or nominal discount rates are to be used.

Reliability issues

The data required to perform accurate calculations are often incomplete or unavailable. As stated in the above section, various costs surrounding the operation, maintenance and repair of building structures are required. However, owing to the time periods under consideration in the lifecycle-costing exercise, reliable data may not have been collated. For example, if a new boiler design is being considered there will be an expected life, however, since the boiler will not have been used in practice, over this length of time this lifespan may be completely inaccurate. Previous research has established large variations in the expected life of even simple building components, such as window frames (Ashworth, 1996). Consequently, great care is required when forecasting such replacement and repair costs. Published guides should be used where appropriate and are published by organisations including:

- Royal Institution of Chartered Surveyors, Building Cost Information Service
- Property Services Agency
- Housing Association Property Mutual
- Building Research Establishment.

Information that the client may have amassed over time should not be overlooked, and indeed may prove very reliable for the particular application. Forecasting includes inherent risks. However, these are compounded by a lack of readily available data for practitioners to use in lifecycle-costing analysis. Practitioners and clients may feel that complete lifecycle costing for contractors' proposed schemes in D&B is not always appropriate. This need does not preclude the use of lifecycle costing as a technique to focus on particular items within the design. This information, if presented in a standardised format, could be either added to the capital cost or converted to a score for 'efficiency' on a tender evaluation criteria score sheet. This process would then have the potential to improve the quality of the decision-making process, allowing the client to make a more informed judgement regarding the overall value of the scheme at tender evaluation stage.

Case study

The following case study describes a D&B tender competition that took place during the EPSRC study. It is not intended as a model of best practice, rather as an example of practice in industry. The case study displays how a structured pre-qualification was undertaken followed by a less well-defined lowest capital cost target-mark proposal evaluation. It also shows how contractors often do not believe that their competitors can profitably build a scheme matching the client's criteria for the price submitted. In doing so, it highlights the range of interpretations of the client's needs by the contractor on relatively undeveloped D&B. In addition, it raises the importance that must be given to checking that the schemes submitted satisfactorily fulfil the client's criteria.

Project background

The scheme, a factory and UK base for an American company, was allocated a £3·5 million budget and was let out to tender without client-developed drawings, but a very well-developed performance specification. The intention was to give the contractors maximum flexibility with development. The client used the services of a quantity surveyor to develop the detailed performance specification. As part of the data collection strategy, documentary analysis was undertaken, and individual and group interviews were held with both the employer's agent and a representative of a contracting organisation who tendered on the project. At the time of interview, the contract was on the verge of being awarded to another contractor than the one interviewed.

The consultants commenced by advertising the scheme in accordance with OJEC regulations. This resulted in a longlist of tenderers that was reduced to six. The six contractors then underwent a pre-qualification process. In the preliminary enquiry they were furnished with details of the scheme and were required to complete a qualification questionnaire. The eight criteria were made explicit, although the relative weightings of the criteria were not made explicit to the contractors.

Pre-qualification presentations

In addition to the completed questionnaire, the contractors each gave a one-hour presentation, which gave them the opportunity to outline their case for inclusion on the tender list. Presentations were structured to follow the framework of eight criteria given in the qualification document, and the meeting was intended to provide the opportunity for both sides to ask questions of each other. The contractors provided evidence of successful projects to prove their competence and to be considered for selection. However, the employer's agent recognised that contractors would not include schemes that were not successful as it was not in their interest to do so. As there was no objective mechanism to check previous work, except by providing references, which again could be skewed toward previous positive outcomes, the employer's agent had to force issues in the interview in an attempt to gain a more holistic view.

At this pre-qualification stage, the client was represented by a panel of five people. These included representatives from the client's organisation, the consultants and, in this instance, the local authority. Each panel member scored the contractors independently, and following this an average of the scores was calculated. An exception was the Construction (Design and Management) Regulations 1994 (CDM) compliance criteria, which were not based on a numerical score, but instead treated as an accept/decline binary decision. The four highest-ranking contractors were given the opportunity to tender, while the two bottom-ranking organisations were informed of their failure in this instance. All four successful contractors were furnished with the Employer's Requirements and developed their tender for the scheme.

Proposal presentations and evaluation

Following submission of the contractor's proposals, contractors were then assessed by the client's consultants prior to a second stage of presentations. The presentation process allows the contractors to illustrate how their proposal meets the design brief, in addition to providing an opportunity for them to draw attention to unique and innovative facets of the scheme. The client's consultants developed an evaluation panel to consider the schemes. Twelve people were incorporated in the panel, including various stakeholders from the local authority, client team and the consultants. All individuals were furnished with the relative criteria that the contractors had been given to base their proposals on. In addition, all individuals were encouraged to ask questions of the contractors. Two individuals were given the task of marking the scheme following discussion with the entire panel to give an element of consensus between those involved. The information sheet shown in Figure 7.6 was given to all 12 members involved in the evaluation. In addition, the straightforward ranking sheet for contractor's proposals is shown in Figure 7.7.

The scoring of the proposals at this stage was less structured than at the pre-qualification stage. The schemes were ultimately deemed either compliant or non-compliant. No explicit price/quality mechanism was used to balance competing strengths and weaknesses of the schemes. The employer's agent, who was ultimately in charge of the evaluation process, did not deem this level of detail necessary, as in his view the quality mechanism was satisfied if the scheme was compliant, as the contractors

---

When reviewing the individual presentations, it may prove helpful to bear in mind some of the fundamental requirements of the design brief

1. The client is a subsidiary of a large American corporation and has an international reputation for the design and provision of specialist communication systems throughout the world. The new building must, therefore, present a 'high-tech' appearance in keeping with the company's business activities.

2. Accommodation is to comprise approximately 6000 m^2 split equally between office and production facilities.

3. Particular attention will need to be paid to the design of:

   (a) the main entrance and reception area – open and airy/two-storey with open-plan staircase
   (b) quality of executive offices and conference rooms
   (c) quality and flexibility of office accommodation
   (d) staff facilities
   (e) quality of environment in production areas, e.g. natural lighting
   (f) layout of related areas, e.g.:

      (i) executive offices – secure, self-contained and close to main entrance
      (ii) operations/development etc. – adjacent to production areas
      (iii) meeting rooms – accessible to all areas
      (iv) staff accommodation – distributed throughout
      (v) production areas – flexible workspace accessible to development/engineering/operations/quality control/loading
      (vi) information technology – centrally located
      (vii) loading, goods in/out – easy access to production.

4. In terms of the overall site layout, particular attention will need to be paid to:

   (a) provision made for future expansion of the premises to 8000 m^2
   (b) provision made for car parking – 180 initially, with space for 240
   (c) separate access for directors and visitor traffic
   (d) provision of helicopter pad
   (e) landscaping
   (f) security
   (g) provision for access on to remainder of land to the north.

5. A life expectancy, without the need for major maintenance works, of at least 40 years is required – choice of materials, service provision and construction format will be important.

Figure 7.6. Project information given to evaluation panel

New premises

Design presentations   Date:

Comments by _____

Order of presentation	Contractor	Ranking 1st – 4th	Comments (best and worst aspects)
1	A		
2	B		
3	C		
4	D		

Figure 7.7. Individual proposal evaluation matrix

had previously been pre-qualified. This means that the lowest capital cost compliant bidder is deemed the overall provider of best value. When asked whether such criteria as functionality, aesthetics and lifecycle costing could have been dealt with more objectively by means of an evaluation matrix as presented in previous sections, the consultant in overall control of the process replied that:

'The long-term robustness of the schemes was ensured by the requirements of the performance specification, as long as that was complied with there was no problem. As long as the schemes complied with what we had asked for, we were quite happy to award the contract to the lowest bidder. In this instance the lowest bidder was not compliant, so the contract went to the second lowest bidder, or the lowest cost compliant bidder.'

This means that this particular project is an example of a relatively pure D&B scheme, where the client was happy to accept the lowest bidder providing the scheme was acceptable. As three of the schemes were acceptable, it simply became a question of selecting the lowest capital cost bid. The relative differences between the bids were not deemed important, as all of them were acceptable to the client.

Compliancy issues

The contractor who was interviewed tendered a sum of £5·8 million for the scheme, and believed that this level of pricing, at £2·3 million over the disclosed budget, was justified to fulfil the client's needs. The contractor did not believe that those contractors who bid at a level close to the budgetary figure could produce a scheme that met the client's specification and requirements without losing money.

However, it should be noted that the contractor included in his scheme a 20% size increase for circulation space and mechanical and electrical housing, as he believed this was needed to fulfil the client's needs. The contractor's submission was very detailed and utilised a 'striking' design, as the client had requested this in his requirements. The contractor submitted a list of optional cost savings that the contractor argued could be used to reduce the tendered sum to £3·5 million, although this was not explicitly stated in the tender documents. The options included various alternatives, for example, eliminating the 20% size increase for modification of the mechanical and electrical specification.

The contractor had a great conviction that the submission by another contractor that was currently pending acceptance was non-compliant. So great was his belief that he accused the employer's agent of not following the issued tender guidelines, which forbid the employer's agent from allowing non-compliant bids to be accepted. Despite these objections from the contractor, the employer's agent believed that the submission was compliant in meeting the Employer's Requirements. Although the submission was more 'modest', for example in the cladding materials used, all the checks and post-tender discussions and clarifications had, for the employer's agent, established its compliance. The contractor remained convinced that the bid must have been non-compliant and offered additional information to substantiate this belief. Shortly after the tender process, the contractor had taken over the mechanical and electrical company that had been used by all firms tendering for the project. In doing so, the contractor had uncovered evidence stating that some companies in the tender competition had bid on the basis of a smaller mechanical and electrical building than that requested by the client. Nevertheless, the employer's agent remained unconvinced that the bid was non-compliant.

A major question is how much information is required from the contractor for the client to ensure that the bid is compliant? The more information the better, yet requiring all bidders to submit very detailed schemes increases the overall tender cost and time required. This is where a two-stage process, utilising considerable design development in the second stage with one contractor, provides benefits. This mechanism allows both sides to become aware of the finer detail of the project and take account of the associated risks. It is always in the client's best interests to scrutinise the scheme offered in as much detail as possible. Although it is accepted that the Employer's Requirements and Contractor's Proposals documents change form as they develop from tender to contractual documents, they should mirror each other in their description of what is required and how that will be fulfilled. Jannsens (1991) states that:

> The Contractor's Proposals complement the Employer's Requirements, and should be checked to ensure that no discrepancy exists between the two documents. Together the documents should contain sufficient drawings and specification details to describe the precise nature of every element of the proposed project, or where this is impractical, the documents should define the standards or parameters that are to apply in the subsequent design development.
>
> (p. 21)

The belief that it is in the contractor's interests to keep the specification vague is, for Jannsens, a strategy that can backfire, as without a specification proving a benchmark of quality, the contractor may be unable to argue that the product provided is of a reasonable standard.

Logically, this line of argument leads to the question of precedence between the Employer's Requirements and the Contractor's Proposals. For Turner (1995), the Contractor's Proposals take precedence, although he cautions against any type of approval over and above *appearing* to meet the client's requirements:

While the employer should examine and assess the tender, if needs be commenting on it and negotiating any amendments, he should not formally approve its detailed contents. If he does, he may well be undermining his own position, if a question of design liability arises. He should certainly point out any divergences from his requirements that are not acceptable to him, because the Contractor's Proposals override the Employer's Requirements once they become contract documents . . . Where it becomes impossible for the employer to shrug off complicity in the contractor's design is over matters such as layout, room heights and general massing of buildings. In questions such as space, function and impact he must be aware under this type of contract, as under any other, of what he is being offered, and so must be held to accept it knowingly. Equally, although not with such precision, he should be aware of the broad standards of quality of what is being offered . . . There are thus areas where the employer may not and others where he may plead ignorance if a post-contract dispute arises. In the former, the broad issues, it is imperative that the employer should check his requirements are being fully met in the Contractor's Proposals and that there is no divergence, over which the latter documents would be definitive. But even in the latter, the narrow issues, the employer is held by the framework of the Contractor's Proposals, so that he can dispute only departures from the framework and not developments within it. He can instruct a change over any issue, but the resulting financial adjustment may go against him.

(pp. 65–66)

For Jannsens, the rules for determining the precedence of the Contractor's Proposals are not so straightforward. The third recital is again an important issue; the employer has checked the Contractor's Proposals and is satisfied that they appear to meet his requirements. However, clause 2.5.1 of JCT 1981 is cited as it requires the contractor to use reasonable skill and care in developing the Contractor's Proposals. Jannsens (1991) argues that the Contractor's Proposals take precedence where the issue is obvious, for example, where there is a discrepancy over finishes, and the Contractor's Proposals contained a clearly stated finished schedule. However, for more subtle differentiation, such as where the Employer's Requirements contained a performance specification stating compliance with Chartered Institution of Building Services Engineers' (CIBSE) guidelines, and the Contractor's Proposals although specific did not comply with the guidelines, the question would have to be asked whether the contractor used reasonable skill and care; if not, he would be in breach.

Whatever the subtleties of the contractual machinery employed, the above underlines the importance of scrutinising the Contractor's Proposals. In addition, it makes clear the importance of the contractor checking clearly the Employer's Requirements document. A director of a regional contracting organisation makes this point during an interview:

> 'What happens today is that the contract form is amended such that discrepancies within the documents fall to be our responsibility. In the old days when there was a discrepancy within the Employers' Requirements you got paid, today you don't and there's a consequence to this. You spend a lot more time trying to find out what those discrepancies are before we sign on the dotted line, so that we don't cop for the money later.'

This underlines the client's use of D&B as a risk-transferred traditional contract. The same contractor continued in a similar vein:

> 'Our bid team consists of two estimators in Birmingham and two estimators in Nottingham. We also have a professional called a bid manager at both ends of the business and that's his sole responsibility, looking at preparing Contractor's Proposals, looking at bid documentation and trying to find any discrepancies or loopholes in them that we need to close.'

Having a well-resourced approach to this issue allows the organisation to attempt to deal with the discrepancies within the tender period as proposed in the majority of tender guides. A contractor made the following remark when interviewed on this issue:

> 'We actually write technical query sheets, send those to the employers' agent during the tender time and get answers back wherever possible. You don't get them all back, depends who you are working with, some you do, some you don't, and those you don't you have to qualify.'

In contrast to some contractors interviewed who withheld problems with the Employer's Requirements, this example shows how a well-structured approach is aimed at alleviating any problems, although the response often does not come in the tender period.

Continuing with the specifics of the case study, the data show that the presence of external funding bodies added increased pressure on the consultants to conduct a swift evaluation and contract award. For example, the project in question included several funding bodies who applied pressure to conclude matters swiftly. As stated, in this instance the employer's agent was convinced that the bid pending acceptance was compliant. The contractor contesting the compliance stated that his bid was so explicit in regard to what it included that it removed all risk from the client. The contractor argued that the employer's agent should repeat the tender competition as the contractor was so sure that the rules stated in the tender documents had been breached. While reiterating his belief that the tender pending acceptance was compliant, the employer's agent stated that if the tender competition needed to be repeated again the project would probably not go ahead as the funders need to meet time-frames was so strong.

The contractor interviewed made the point that in his tender he had made the cost savings very explicit, thereby directing the client to the possible cost savings, as opposed to attempting to hide them in what would appear a compliant bid. This draws attention to the fact that it is the compliant bid, and its associated price, that forms primary focus of analysis. While alternatives are important, it is the compliant bid which is used in evaluation.

In this instance, the problem of scrutinising the detail of the documentation was magnified by the degree of complexity and range of information provided. Although the tender documents for the project stated the level of detail required, contractors' bids vary on this issue, making evaluation difficult.

An interesting dimension of the contractor's belief that the tender pending acceptance was not compliant is demonstrated by a previous scheme between the client and the contractor interviewed. In this example, the contractor was awarded the contract, yet another tendering contractor argued that the contractor could not meet the client's requirements for the sum tendered. The unsuccessful contractor in this instance visited the site and believed that the completed scheme did not adequately meet the Employer's Requirements. This highlights one of the major issues with pure D&B; that the client's needs can be met in a multitude of different ways. The contractor's reference point, in such a tender competition, is the Employer's Requirements document and interaction with the client, which varies between clients and projects. Whereas the client is characterised in many texts as diligently evaluating the Contractor's Proposals based on various criteria, and then choosing the most balanced bid that contains the most appropriate facets, the reality is that the client is often not too particular about the intricacies of each design and simply establishes a baseline of compliance and then chooses on cost. As in this example, the realisation that the overall strengths and weaknesses of the different schemes may not be taken account of in the evaluation process is complicated by the fact that design itself is a subjective issue.

The study has clarified an important relationship between the client's needs, the documentary representation of his needs, and the final tendered scheme. When using pure D&B it would seem that it is difficult to encapsulate the client's predilection to certain designs in the Employer's Requirements. In some respects, a client cannot define what he likes until he has seen it; objective and solution are separate entities. Therefore, the client evaluates the solution to his objectives when he evaluates the Contractor's Proposals. When the contractor and client do not liaise during the tender period, the first time that the client will see the design is following submission. This means that the first feedback that the client can give comes at the end of the tender process during the competitive element. Thus, the contractor cannot take account of the client's feedback to his scheme development during evolution of his proposals. This can lead to a limited use of the tender stage and, ultimately, a wasted opportunity for both contractor and client. Mid-tender meetings are important in this regard and can aid direction of the contractor's scheme development, although, again, contractors need to be able to believe that their competitive advantage will not be lost to their competitors.

As stated, in pure D&B the contractor can meet the client's requirements in numerous ways. A large degree of freedom in the Employer's Requirements results in a large degree of variance in the nature of the schemes and associated costs. What the analysis makes clear is the need for the contractor to be made aware, or indeed actively make himself aware, in the most explicit way of the relativity of the client's objectives. This principle is also used by proactive successful contractors to challenge the client's needs, and consultant designs on developed D&B.

In the case study example, the contractor interviewed realised during proposal development that the project could not be built for the budget amount. This left him in a dilemma over what course of action to take. The design element had already devoured valuable time, so a radical rethink was not an option. It was decided that contacting the employer's agent was not a valid option either, as it would not be perceived favourably. Thus, the contractor decided to continue with the design development he believed was necessary to meet the client's requirements and exceed budget as required to ensure the client's needs were met. This lack of communication between the contractor and the client team was a serious problem. Had the tender process been characterised by a more open form of communication and dialogue between both parties, the contractor may have developed what the employer's agent would have perceived as a more appropriate design. As previously stated, the EPSRC data suggest that this lack of communication at tender stage is a common problem, one principal reason is that contractors feel that discussions may result in dissemination of their ideas to other tendering contractors. In certain situations their ideas may be given to the contractor who is eventually awarded the contract. Clients may find it difficult to avoid facilitating some transfusion between contractors. Public clients have generally developed accountable tendering procedures as their use of public funds requires. However, this is also commonly stated as a catalyst for a lack of openness and communication. Despite calling for extensions of time in the tender period, which were denied, the contractor interviewed continued without interaction with the client team. As the contractor states, the extra time required for design development prior to being able to take-off quantities in such pure D&B is often not reflected in the time allowed for tender.

Summary

This chapter has attempted to draw together themes developed throughout the book and apply them in a practical context. The various types of D&B, previously presented as points on a continuum of pre-contractor design and specification development, were shown with corresponding variations of tender competition. Extensive use of practitioners' views were used to contextualise the chapter. Models of contractor selection were then presented. These were used to clarify the processes involved in D&B tender strategies and can act as a foundation for developing and communicating procedures in actual projects. For reasons of clarity, the integration of value management and lifecycle-costing techniques were illustrated in separate sections and provide a resource for those wishing to incorporate these tools into tender evaluation mechanisms. Finally, a case study was presented to illustrate the views of practitioners involved in the whole process of D&B evaluation, and stressed the need to thoroughly check the detail of Contractor's Proposals and faster communication during scheme development.

References

Akintoye, A. (1994). Design and build: a survey of construction contractors' views. *Construction Management and Economics*, **12**, 155–193.

Akintoye, A. and Fitzgerald, E. (1995). Design and build: a survey of architect's views. *Engineering, Construction and Architectural Management*, **2**, No. 1, 27–44.

Ashworth, A. (1996). *Pre-contract Studies — Development Economics, Tendering and Estimating.* Longman, Harlow.

Ashworth, A. and Hogg, K. (2000). *Added value in design and construction.* Longman, Harlow.

Baker, M. and Osraah, S. (1985). How do the customers choose a contractor? *Building*, May, 30–31.

Bannock, G., Baxter, R. and Davis, E. (1998). *Dictionary of Economics*, 6th edn. Penguin, London.

Banwell, H. (1964). *The Placing and Management of Contracts for Building and Civil Engineering Work.* HMSO, London.

Begg, D., Fischer, S. and Dornbusch, R. (1994). *Economics*, 4th edn. McGraw-Hill, London.

Bennett, J., Pothecary, E. and Robinson, G. (1996). *Designing and Building a World Class Industry.* Centre for Strategic Studies in Construction, University of Reading.

Bruce, T. (2000). What is the Role of Ethics in Design–Build Projects? *Journal of Professional Issues in Engineering Education and Practice*, July.

Chappell, D. (1994). Architect's Legal Position on D&B: Special Report on Design and Build. *Architect's Journal*, Mar., 9th edn, London.

Chartered Institute of Building (CIOB) (1988). *Code of Estimating Practice, Supplement No.2: Design and Build*. CIOB, Ascot.

Chevin, D. (1993). Fitting the Bill. *Building — Design and Build Supplement*, July, 4.

Construction Industry Board (CIB) (1997). *Code of Practice for the Selection of Main Contractors*. Working Group 3, CIB. Thomas Telford, London.

Construction Industry Development Agency (CIDA) (1995). *Prequalification Criteria for Contractors*. CIDA, Sydney.

Construction Industry Institute (CIIA) (1996). *Constructability Manual*. CIIA, Adelaide.

Construction Industry Research and Information Association (CIRIA) (1998). *Selecting Contractors by Value*. CIRIA, London.

Craig, R. (2000). Re-engineering the tender code for construction works. *Construction Management and Economics*, **18**, No. 1, 91–100

Crisp, R. (2000). *Routledge philosophy guidebook to Mill on Utilitarianism*. Routledge, London.

Denning, J. (1992). Design–Build Goes Public. *Proceedings of the Institution of Civil Engineers, Civil Engineering*, July, 76–79.

Economic Development Committee for Building (1967). *Action on the Banwell Report*. HMSO, London.

Egan, Sir J. (1998). *Rethinking Construction*. Report of the Construction Task Force on the Scope for Improving the Quality and Efficiency of UK Construction, Department of the Environment, Transport and the Regions, London.

Emmerson, H. (1962). *A Survey of Problems Before the Construction Industry: a report prepared for the Ministry of Works*. HMSO, London.

Farrow, J. J. (1993). Tendering — An Applied Science. *Occasional Paper No.1*. Chartered Institute of Building, Ascot.

Farrow, J. J. and Main, F. R. (1996). Use and Abuse of the Code of Procedure for Single Stage Selective Tendering. *Construction Paper No. 70*, Chartered Institute of Building, Ascot.

Fredrickson, K. (1998). Design Guidelines for Design–Build Projects. *Journal of Management in Engineering*. ASCE Press Ltd, New York.

Friedman, M. (1982). *Capitalism and Freedom*. The University of Chicago Press, Chicago.

Green, S. (1992). *A SMART methodology for value management*. Chartered Institute of Building, Ascot.

Griffith, A. (1989). *Design–Build Procurement and Buildability.* Technical Information Service Paper, No. 112, Chartered Institute of Building, Ascot.

Griffith, A. and Sidwell, A. C. (1995). *Constructability in Building and Engineering Projects.* Macmillan, Basingstoke.

Harp, W. D. (1988). *Historical Background Low Bid Concept.* Annual General Meeting of the Task Force, Denver. Cited in Herbsman, Z. and Ellis, R. (1992). Multiparameter Bidding System — Innovation in Contract Administration. *Journal of Construction Engineering and Management.* ASCE Press Ltd, New York.

Harvey, J. (1996). *Urban Land Economics,* 4th edn. Macmillan, Basingstoke.

Hatush, Z. and Skitmore, M. (1997). Criteria for Contractor Selection. *Construction Management and Economics,* **15**, 19–38.

Herbsman, Z. and Ellis, R. (1992). Multiparameter Bidding System — Innovation in Contract Administration. *Journal of Construction Engineering and Management.* ASCE Press Ltd, New York.

Hill, R. M. (2000). Better Building — Integrating the Supply Chain: A Guide for Clients and their Consultants. *BRE Digest 450.* British Research Establishment, Watford.

HM Treasury (1997). *Central Unit on Procurement (CUP) No. 56 Debriefing.* HMSO, London.

HM Treasury (1999a). *Procurement Guidance No.3: Appointment of Consultants and Contractors.* The Stationery Office, London.

HM Treasury (1999b). *Procurement Guidance No. 5: Procurement Strategies.* The Stationery Office, London.

Holt, G. D. (1995). *A Methodology for Predicting the Performance Potential of Construction Contractors.* PhD Thesis, Wolverhampton University.

Holt, G. D. (1998). Which Contractor Selection Methodology? *International Journal of Project Management,* **16**, No. 3, 153–164.

Holt, G. D., Olomolaiye, P. O. and Harris, F. C. (1996). Tendering Procedures, Contractual Arrangements and Latham: The Contractors' View. *Engineering, Construction and Architectural Management,* **1**, No. 2, 97–115.

Janssens, D. E. L. (1991). *Design–Build Explained.* Macmillan, Basingstoke.

Joint Contracts Tribunal (JCT) (2002). *Practice Note Six. Main Contract Tendering.* Royal Institute of British Architects, London.

Kelly, J. and Male, S. (1998). *The Value Management Benchmark: A Good Practice Framework for Clients and Practitioners.* Thomas Telford, London.

Kelly, J. and Male, S. (2002). *Value Management of Construction Projects*. Blackwell Science, Oxford.

Knight, A. D., Griffith, A., Sharples, S. and King, A. P. (2002). *Improved Tender Evaluation in Design and Build Construction Projects*. EPSRC Final Report No. GR/N02689/01.

Latham, Sir M. (1994). *Constructing the Team*. Final Report on Joint Review of Procurement and Contractual Arrangements in the UK Construction Industry, HMSO, London.

Mosey, D. (1998). *Design and Build in Action*. Chandos Publishing Ltd, Oxford.

National Audit Office (NAO) (2001). *Modernising Construction*. Report by the Comptroller and Auditor General, HC87 Session 2000–2001. The Stationery Office, London.

National Joint Consultative Committee for Building (NJCC) (1995). *Code of Procedure for Selective Tendering for Design and Build*. Royal Institute of British Architects, London.

National Joint Consultative Committee for Building (NJCC) (1996a). *Code of Procedure for Single Stage Selective Tendering*. Royal Institute of British Architects, London.

National Joint Consultative Committee for Building (NJCC) (1996b). *Code of Procedure for Two Stage Selective Tendering*. Royal Institute of British Architects, London.

Oliver, A. (2000). Value, Ontological Status Of. *Concise Routledge Encyclopedia of Philosophy*. Routledge, London.

Palaneeswaran, E., Kumaraswamy, M. and Tam, P. W. M. (1999). Comparing Approaches to Contractor Selection for Design and Build Projects. *Proceedings of the CIB W55 and W65 Joint Triennial Symposium, Customer Satisfaction: A Focus for Research and Practice*, Cape Town, 5–10 Sept.

Palaneeswaran, E. and Kumaraswamy, M. (2001). Recent advances and proposed improvements in contractor prequalification methodologies. *Building and Environment*, **36**, 73–87.

Pasquire, C. and Swaffield, L. (2002). Life-cycle/Whole-life Costing. In Kelly, J., Morledge, R. and Wilkinson, S. (eds), *Best Value in Construction*. Blackwell Publishing, Oxford.

Pearson, A. (1999). Chain Reaction. *Building*, 12 March, 54–55.

Potter, K. J. and Sanvido, V. (1994). Design/Build Prequalifcation System. *Journal of Management in Engineering*, **10**, 48–56.

Ray, R. S., Hornibrook, J. and Skitmore, M. (1999). Ethics in Tendering: a survey of Australian opinion and practice. *Construction Management and Economics*, **17**, 139–153.

Robinson, C. (1997). Procuring Profits. *Building*, 13 June, 38.

Royal Institution of Chartered Surveyors (RICS) (1996). *The Procurement Guide: a guide to the development of an appropriate building procurement strategy*. RICS, London.

Royal Institution of Chartered Surveyors (RICS) (1999). *The Surveyors' Construction Handbook — Section 2: Life Cycle Costing*. RICS, London.

Russell, J. S. (1996). *Contractor's Prequalification: Choosing the best constructor and avoiding constructor failure*. ASCE Press Ltd, New York.

Siddiqui, A. W. (1996). Novation: and its comparison with common forms of building procurement. *Construction Papers No. 60*. Chartered Institute of Building, Ascot.

Simon Committee (1944). *The Placing and Management of Buliding Contracts*. HMSO, London.

Strauss, A. and Corbin, J. M. (1998). *Basics of Qualitative Research. Grounded Theory Procedures and Techniques*. Sage, London.

Turner, D. F. (1995). *Design and Build Contract Practice*, 2nd edn. Longman, Harlow.

Wong, C. H., Holt, G. D. and Harris, P. (1999). UK Construction Clients' Opinions of the Contractor Selection Process. *Proceedings of ARCOM Conference*, Liverpool John Moores University, 15–17 Sept, Volume 2.

Zechman, E. (2000). Ethics in the Design–Build Process. *Journal of Professional Issues in Engineering Education and Practice*, July.

Index